After Disbelief

After Disbelief

On Disenchantment, Disappointment, Eternity, and Joy

ANTHONY T. KRONMAN

Yale UNIVERSITY PRESS

New Haven and London

Published with assistance from the Mary Cady Tew
Memorial Fund.

Yale University Press books may be purchased in quantity for
educational, business, or promotional use. For information, please
e-mail sales.press@yale.edu (U.S. office) or sales@yaleup.co.uk
(U.K. office).

Set in Minion type by Integrated Publishing Solutions, Grand
Rapids, Michigan.
Printed in the United States of America.

Library of Congress Control Number: 2021943666
ISBN 978-0-300-25992-6 (hardcover : alk. paper)

A catalogue record for this book is available from the British
Library.

This paper meets the requirements of ANSI/NISO Z39.48-1992
(Permanence of Paper).

10 9 8 7 6 5 4 3 2 1

For Owen Fiss
That my hero is my friend—how lucky am I!

But superstition, like belief, must die,
And what remains when disbelief has gone?

—FROM "CHURCH GOING," BY PHILIP LARKIN

Contents

Introduction
God in the Closet

MY PARENTS HAD AN ALLERGY to God. They thought the idea a fable for credulous fools. They warned me against the dangers of religion and banished God from the family table. They locked him in a closet, where his malign power could be safely contained. And there he remained, hidden from view, though never forgotten, and more than a little beguiling.

My father was Jewish, my mother Christian. They came from different backgrounds but shared a contempt for religion in all its organized forms. From my earliest days, they taught me that religion is for weak-minded people who are intolerant of others and afraid of the truth—like the ignorant rubes H. L. Mencken savaged in his dispatches from the Scopes Monkey Trial.[1] They despised the things that people do in the name of God. They encouraged me to think of religion as a poison that must be avoided at all costs.

Not every reference to religion was ruthlessly barred from my home. Like our neighbors, we celebrated Christmas with glee. My father was in fact something of a Christmas nut, despite his Jewish upbringing. I went with him every December to pick a tree the first day the lot was open. He always chose a big one with a perfect top for the star that had been packed away since the Christmas before, then had the tree dressed with cotton that was meant to look like snow—New England in Southern California.

But Christmas had nothing to do with religion. No one in my family ever remarked that we were celebrating the birth of Jesus, except to note that he had been a very kind man, who happened, for circumstantial reasons, to have been born in a manger, and always with the qualification that only superstitious people believe he is the Son of God.

The same was true of Passover, which we celebrated less regularly and with distinctly less enthusiasm. Most years, we skipped it entirely. On the infrequent occasions we had a Seder, it was never at home. We always went across town to my Aunt Rose's. I had a good enough time, I suppose, though it didn't compare with Christmas. But Passover had nothing to do with religion either. It was just a family meal with some relatives I rarely saw otherwise and a few peculiar rituals we hurried through to get to the food at the end. I was an adult before I knew what the meal means.

Growing up, I had Jewish and Christian friends. I went to their bar mitzvahs and confirmation parties. I danced and flirted like the other teenagers. But I was always looking in from the outside, a little apprehensively, at something I'd been warned was bad for my health. As some point, these experiences moved me to reflect in a more self-conscious way on my own identity. Who or what was I? A Christian or a Jew or both? Perhaps neither?

As best I can recall, the only time the question had come up before was when, as a nine- or ten-year-old, I was threatened on the walk home from school by an older bully who lived down the street. He pushed me and called me a kike. I'm not sure I'd heard the word before, but I knew it wasn't good, like the little boy in Salinger's story "Down at the Dinghy," who hears his father called a kike and is very upset because he thinks it means one of those things you fly on a string with a tail.[2]

I told my parents about the incident. They argued fiercely. It was one of the few times I can remember their ever arguing in my presence.

My father thought the slur absurd. There was nothing Jewish about me, he said. I never went to temple and didn't know a single word of Hebrew. My mother angrily replied that it made no difference what *I* did or didn't do. The important thing was how other people saw me. In their eyes, she said, a half-Jew is a Jew. And then she cursed the whole tribe of anti-Semites, about whom, I later learned, she knew a thing or two.

In the years that followed, the question of identity came back to me, from time to time. When I was thirteen, and going to my friends' bar mitzvahs and confirmation parties, I asked my parents again, more deliberately this time, whether I was Jewish or Christian or neither or both. It seemed fair, I said, that I get to answer the question myself, rather than leaving it up to the bully down the street.

My mother, in particular, was not unsympathetic to my youthful confusion. She had nothing but contempt for religion herself, but thought it reasonable that I be allowed to make up my own mind about it. She proposed an experiment to settle the matter.

We would go to a different service each week, she said. At the end I could pick the one I liked best. For the time being at least, that would answer the question of my identity. It seemed like a rational procedure. My father was not much interested in the whole business but acquiesced in my mother's plan—as he generally did when it came to questions of religion.

The experiment lasted a week. My mother took me and my younger brother to an Episcopal Mass at an imposing

church in West Los Angeles. The service was long and confus-
ing. Everyone but me seemed to know what was happening.
My dress pants itched. The next Sunday I went to the beach
instead. I suspect that is what my mother wanted. Being a good
parent meant inoculating me against deforming diseases, like
polio. Religion fell into the same category.

My parents were intelligent atheists. They had a battery of reasons for their disbelief. But as I eventually discovered, their
disdain for religion was not the product of reasoned reflection
alone. Nor did it come to them only as mature adults. I learned
from the stories they told me about their own childhood that
religion had once been a tremendous force in their lives whose
influence they had both fought hard to escape.

    My father grew up on the Lower East Side in New York
City in the early years of the twentieth century. His parents,
Ignatz and Julia, had come to America in the 1890s from the
country that became Hungary after the First World War. Ignatz was a tailor and Julia a seamstress, like many of the Jews
who lived in the neighborhood where they settled. They had
five children, including my father, who seems to have been an
especially bright child.

    In 1918, my father's parents sent him to Cincinnati to
study at the Hebrew Union College. He graduated six years
later with a rabbinical degree and for two years after that offi-
ciated at the Washington Hebrew Congregation in Washington, D.C. Then, for reasons he never fully explained, to me at
least, he left the rabbinate and practicing Judaism altogether.

    After a brief stint in his brother Sam's furniture-making
business in New York, my father moved to Los Angeles in 1935,
where he had a decades-long career as a radio and television
writer. In 1940, his friend Louella Parsons introduced him to
my mother at Schwab's Drugstore on Sunset Boulevard. They

married soon after. My mother was eighteen years younger and strikingly beautiful. In the 1930s she had been an actress at Warner Brothers, where she starred in several films with Ronald Reagan before leaving for reasons that also were never clearly explained, though I suspect sexual predation had something to do with it.

When my father was there as a student in the early 1920s, the Hebrew Union College was a hotbed of progressive Jewish thought—of Bible criticism and other "scientific" approaches to the study of religion that were eating like an acid into the heart of orthodox belief. Reform Judaism had come to America in the 1840s. It was a marginal phenomenon in Europe but flourished here. Its relaxed approach to orthodoxy was well-suited to the conditions of American life and appealed to many Jews eager to assimilate. The Hebrew Union College was the flagship of the Reform movement in America. Its curriculum and culture challenged traditional beliefs with gleeful abandon. At a dinner for the first graduating class in 1883, the menu included soft-shell crabs and frogs' legs. It was called the Trefa Banquet.[3]

I suspect that when my father arrived at the Hebrew Union College at the age of eighteen, he was already less than perfectly deferential to established authority. (A note in the registrar's files from his first year at the college states that my father's "conduct in Dr. Newmark's class is not such as it should be and that the Faculty sincerely hopes that the cause for the complaint will soon be corrected.")

Six years of study in an intellectually adventurous environment must have reinforced every rebellious bone in my father's body. By the time he graduated at twenty-four, he had read Nietzsche and other dangerous writers. He had become a "free-thinker" (his phrase). Ordained as a rabbi and certified to preach, he thought of religion as ethics in disguise—a system of perfectly reasonable moral teachings hidden behind an accumulation of absurd superstitions and nonsensical practices that serve no rational purpose at all.

Perhaps my father went to Cincinnati disposed to such a view, rebelliously inclined against the Old-World orthodoxy of his immigrant parents. Or perhaps it first took shape in his early twenties, under the influence of the critical ideas he absorbed from his teachers, who stood at the far end of liberal Jewish thought. In any case, it was the view of religion my father held for the rest of his life.

It did not inspire him to become a strident critic of religion (as my mother was). He saw religion as a sop for simpleminded people who need to have their ethics dressed in rituals and incantations to bolster their commitment to behave as they ought. But my father assigned no independent value to religion. Mostly, he just lost interest in it. Debating religious ideas seemed to him a colossal waste of time. Much better, he thought, to spend it weeding our vegetable garden.

My mother, by contrast, was not disinterested in religion. She actively *hated* it. She had experienced religion as a profoundly destructive force in her own life and spoke with ferocious passion about its scarring effects.

My maternal grandmother, Viola, was born in 1893 on a farm in Missouri. She held the terrifying beliefs about heaven and hell that were preached by the primitive evangelical Christianity of the old-stock Americans among whom she was raised.[4] She changed her religious affiliation several times later in life. In her mid-fifties, she converted to Roman Catholicism. My mother's mother remained a religious fanatic until the day she died.

When my mother was growing up in Los Angeles in the

1920s, my grandmother dragged her to countless revivals and prayer meetings in churches and open-air tents. My mother heard Amy Semple McPherson preach at the Angelus Temple in Echo Park and saw her perform the faith-healing miracles for which she was famous. As a child, my mother was taught that God is a vigilant presence, always there, always judging, able to see her innermost thoughts and ready to punish her for the wicked ones (of which she knew she had many). Religion was, for her, a region of mystery and fear—inexorable, irrational, and cruel.

In time, my mother managed to escape the pull of religion through a nearly super-human effort to see and judge things for herself—a liberation she won on her own. Later in life, looking back at the world she had left behind, my mother saw religion as the symbol and cause of all the ignorance and bigotry that trapped nearly everyone else in her family. My mother's hatred of religion became the most powerful expression of the pride she took in her own improbable victory over the narrow circumstances of her birth. It was the source of the energy with which she defended everything that in her mind stood in opposition to religion—science, tolerance, the pleasure of reading—and of the devotion with which she taught these things to her children.

My father's disdain for religion was cooler than my mother's. He did not feel so damaged by it. He lacked her passion for the subject and deferred to her stronger feelings, which became the norm in my family. But their shared antagonism toward religious ideas and practices, in all their different forms, was a bond between these otherwise remarkably different human beings. They agreed—they simply assumed—that there would be no religion at our table: my father because he had no interest in it and my mother because she viewed God as a monstrous force from which her children must be protected at all costs. And so God was nowhere in my home—except as a danger that was present throughout, like an invisible virus. My parents did their best to shield me from it.

They were only partly successful.

1

The Humanist's God

CHILDREN ARE ATTRACTED to dangerous things. The more they are warned about them, the more curious they become. This is what happened with me and religion.

Early on, I began to wonder why, if religion is so stupid and cruel, millions of people are taken in by it. How can so many people go so badly wrong? Must those who believe in God check their minds at the church door out of respect for the mysteries within? Is religion always the enemy of enlightenment, as my mother said? These questions already engaged me as a child, in a vague and undisciplined way.

I knew, though, that any answer I gave would have to pass the bar of reason. My mother had no respect for those who slavishly defer to the Bible or substitute prayer for thought. That is the real crime of religion, as she saw it. She taught me never to accept any answer on faith or the say-so of other people. My mother was a rationalist. The only views she thought worthy of consideration are those that have been worked out on the basis of reason alone.

She was also a philosopher, temperamentally at least. Far more than my father, who had some academic philosophical training, my mother, who never went to college, was fascinated by questions of the abstract sort that philosophers love to debate. Did the universe have a beginning or has it always existed? Does space come to an end? Where do we human beings stand in the vast order of things? What is the meaning of life?

My mother thought about these questions in a passionate, indeed nearly obsessive way. She read countless books and took courses at our local junior college. She discussed the questions with me at length, on our front steps, in the evening after dinner, when the gardenias were in bloom, with a martini in her hand. It was intoxicating. I have never gotten over the experience.

Among the philosophical questions that interested my mother, the last one seemed to her the most urgent: In light of the fact that we die, do our lives have any enduring meaning at all? My mother eschewed the comforting answers that religion gives to the question. She was determined to do without them. But then what if anything remains to be said?

Sometime in her late forties, my mother came to a resolute answer. She announced that she was an existentialist. She arrived at her view after reading Camus and Sartre in one of her classes at Santa Monica City College. She made it clear to me that even an intelligent child should agree with her conclusions.

We only live for a while, my mother said, and then we die. After death, there is nothing. The only fulfillment we ever find is in this life. We must make what meaning we can of our lives with no help from a God who doesn't exist, and no support from a world that is devoid of purpose or plan.

The meaning of life, she told me, is self-created and short-lived. Even our most intense joys are shadowed by the fact of our irreversible extinction and imminent return to the pointless play of atoms in a godless void. My mother bravely held to this fierce and demanding philosophy until she died at ninety-six.

My mother was an independent-minded person. Her search for answers had led her to Camus and Sartre. I did not fully understand what she was telling me or where her thinking might lead. I was twelve or thirteen at the time. But I felt we were on some dangerous mission together. Her ideas seemed exciting and courageous. More than anything else, I wanted to please and be like her. And so along with her rationalism and philosophical curiosity, I inherited my mother's existentialism, too, and took it with me when I went to college five years later.

My first philosophy seminar was on Sartre's *Being and Nothingness,* a work of immense difficulty that my mother had not read and I was sure would not understand without help from her now better-educated son. I wore my new knowledge as a badge of pride. I was going to be an existentialist of an even higher grade. I would teach my mother how.[1]

But then slowly, over time, my existentialism came undone. It began to seem less compelling. Religion remained for me a subject of special fascination, as it had been since God was locked away in my childhood closet. I wanted to know if there is a rationally defensible sense in which one may say that God exists—contrary to what my mother taught me. It never occurred to me to think that I might find the answer to this question in the teachings of any church. That would have involved an intellectual sacrifice of the kind my mother abhorred. But I came gradually to see the existentialism of Camus and

Sartre, which had once so deeply impressed me, as an inadequate response to certain defining human experiences that religion distortedly reflects, as in a wavy mirror.

Increasingly, their account of the human condition seemed to me thin and unconvincing. My early allegiance to Camus and Sartre gave way, first to one thing, then another, until in late middle age I had arrived at a view of life that has a central place for God, though not one those who are religious in a more conventional sense are likely to recognize or accept. If my life as a whole has a spiritual thread, it connects the fiercely negative idea of God my mother bequeathed to me as a child to the positive if eccentric idea I now hold with equal fervor, though (I like to think) for reasons I can explain even to the most determined disbelievers.

By the time I had arrived at my rational theology and written a long book expounding it, even my close friends thought I was a little mad. It puzzled them that I should be so interested in religion.[2] That I was sympathetic to it made matters worse. That I wound up defending God in any form struck some of them as truly bizarre.

I suspect this is because many of my friends share my mother's views about God and the meaning of life. In the academic circles in which I live and work, the only respectable view of God is that he doesn't exist. The question of the meaning of life is one we have to work out for ourselves in the interval between birth and death. There is no God who directs our decisions, or judges our actions, and no afterlife in which the significance of what we do will be confirmed one way or another.

Of course, even my most adamantly atheistic friends believe that the world will go on for some time after they die. They acknowledge that the meaning of what they do in their

lives rests on the implicit assumption that the world is rela-
tively more lasting than they are—those parts of it, at least, to
which they give their time, energy, and love. If the world dis-
appeared the moment we do, what would be the point of writing books or having children?[3] What nearly all my friends
hotly deny is that the purposefulness and value of their lives
depend on their connection to anything *ever*lasting. This was
my mother's view too.

Many people in the world outside our colleges and uni-
versities see things differently. They believe that to be meaningful in an ultimate sense, their hopes and dreams, and lives
as a whole, must be anchored in a reality that is not merely
more durable than themselves, but absolutely immune to the
vicissitudes of time. Only this can quiet what is for them the
supremely discouraging thought that if everyone and everything to which they are devoted is destined to disappear too,
then their lives have no final, secure goal to guarantee their
significance and value.

In the past, this way of thinking was nearly universal.
The belief that there is an eternal order of some kind, and that
we human beings are connected to it, was so well-supported
by a vast scaffolding of institutions, habits, and ideas that few
even noticed the belief, let alone thought it could be challenged. All the banal routines of life confirmed it. So did the
speculations of philosophers and theologians. The idea that
nothing lasts forever seemed incredible if not insane.

Then, slowly at times, quickly at others, more acutely in
one place than another, this idea became more plausible. It became easier to believe that everything eventually disappears—
even the stars, which once seemed beyond time's reach—and
to disbelieve that the meaning of our lives depends on their connection to something eternal.[4] The process has lasted for more
than half a millennium. It is a great hydraulic force, boundless,

irresistible, cutting every old religious truth loose from its ancient moorings.

This is the meaning of the familiar claim that the world today is disenchanted—that God is dead.[5] Our world is godless not because we have all abandoned the belief that only a connection to eternity can save human life from futility and despair. Many still believe this. It is godless because the presence of an eternal order, natural or supernatural, is no longer so intimately woven into the fabric of everyday life that the existence of this order is as obvious as that of the world itself.

The loss of this sense of obviousness has not destroyed the possibility of belief in God. Nothing could do that. But it has put an unprecedented burden on those who, in the face of this loss, continue to insist that the meaning of life depends on its connection to an eternal reality that is invulnerable to the corrosive power of time.

Those who believe this must now struggle to hold on to their conviction in a world of scientific, literary, and historical "truths" that challenge it at every turn. Many succeed, though their victory is often hard-won. Others give up completely. They resign themselves to disbelief. The liquidation of all the old eternities, banal and refined, that once seemed so palpable and near speeds them along.

This is the setting in which modern atheism flourishes.

The loss of the everyday presence of eternity in the lives of human beings—of the cathedral bell tolling the hours by which those in the market measure their days—gives atheism a credibility it never had before. The critical power of modern ideas provides further support. To many, some version of my mother's view of life now seems the only rational one.

The atheist says that the meaning and value of human life have in truth never depended on our connection to anything eternal. It was always an illusion to think that they do. After a long historical struggle, we now see this with clear eyes. It is enough that the things we admire and love have a (somewhat) longer life than our own. There is no need for them to be connected to an eternal order of any kind, whether in the world or beyond it.

The contrary belief is, in the atheist's view, a crippling superstition. It has long stood in the way of achieving our human potential. To be fully and actively human, we must put this belief aside. We need to reconcile ourselves to the brevity and finality of our existence in time. The death of God is not a catastrophe. It is a liberation.[6]

The most assertive take a further step. They say that all the things we value in life would *lose* their value if our wish to be connected to eternity could be fulfilled. It is the fact that nothing lasts, they say, that gives poignancy and meaning to the short-lived attachments we form. These are meaningful *because* we know they must come to an end. Montaigne and Hume were early if cautious defenders of this view.[7] Camus and Sartre advanced it more aggressively. Martin Hägglund's recent book, *This Life,* is a stirring restatement of what he calls the "secular" view of life. The meaning of the relations we cherish vanishes, Hägglund says, when they are extracted from time and transposed to some imagined condition of life everlasting.[8]

Those who defend this point of view regard themselves as the champions of humanity. They are the prophets of modernity, at home in a godless world that religiously minded men and women naively refuse to accept. They view those who still long for a connection to eternity as backward children.

Atheistic humanism of this aggressive sort is not widely shared. It has the same extravagance as many forms of religious belief. But it represents the most serious intellectual challenge that those who say they believe in God, or even want to, face in our age of disbelief. That is because it harmonizes with many of our scientific and cultural attitudes. It draws strength from these attitudes and reinforces them in turn. It fits the mood of the times. As a result, it has growing appeal among the most enlightened citizens of our increasingly secular world.

But it is wrong. Indeed, it is worse than that. It is inhumane. It misrepresents the human condition and distorts the prospects for a meaningful life. For a rounded picture of the human condition it substitutes a cartoon.

To defeat this brand of militant atheism, it is not enough merely to affirm one's belief in God, even with the greatest sincerity, or to invoke the authority of some sacred tradition or text. All appeals of this kind fall on deaf ears. To the atheist, they are irrational dogmas unworthy of a response.

There is only one way to blunt this attack.

The longing for eternity, which the atheist derides, must be shown to be a constituent element of our humanity, not an avertable threat to it—a feature, not a bug. To defeat the most articulate version of the antireligious dogma that many educated people now accept as the best expression of the highest ideal of life still available to them, humanism must be rescued from the grip of the atheist. It has to be restored to the possession of those who love God without shame. The longing for eternity needs to be put back at the center of the human condition, where it has always been, and still belongs today.

Like other living things, we all eventually die. But we alone *know* we will.

Awareness of our mortality sets us apart. It opens a chasm between us and our animal friends.[9] This knowledge is the starting point of the existentialism my mother embraced as the only alternative she could see to mindless religious belief.

But her existentialism misses something important. It is

true that our knowledge of death is the defining mark of the human condition. But this already assumes an awareness of the distinction between what exists in time and what does not. It presupposes the idea of eternity. And this in turn is connected to the idea of God.

Indeed, the two are more than just connected. They are inseparably joined.

Some think of God in personal terms, as the Children of Abraham do. Others, like the philosophers of pagan antiquity, or many New Age spiritualists, imagine God to be an impersonal force of some kind. Within these broad categories, there are further distinctions. The Unitarian's God is not the Catholic's and both differ from the Muslim's or Jew's. All are radically different from the God of Aristotle's *Metaphysics* and the divine force of Wiccans and Druids.

But these different ideas of God share something important. Each conceives of God as a being or power that does not come into existence and pass away, as you and I do, but endures forever. In the broadest sense, the idea of God, in all its variant forms, *is* the idea of eternity—of someone or something exempt from the whirlwind of time. Even those who deny the existence of God have this idea in mind when they do.

The idea of eternity is at once the condition and consequence of the awareness that we ourselves are mortal. It is both the premise and product of the knowledge that we will die, as distinct from the mere fact that we do. The knowledge of death and the idea of eternity are the two sides of a single coin. They are born together and together make us human.

That we cannot avoid the idea of eternity, any more than we can our awareness of death, does not mean that we are able actually to reach what we imagine lies beyond the limits of time. The idea of eternity does not prove that a deathless order of some kind really exists, let alone is attainable by us. It does not prove the existence of God (as disbelievers of all sorts remind us).

What the idea of eternity *does* do is allow us to form ambitions and engage in pursuits, personal and collective, that cannot be brought to completion in any span of time, however long. It enables us to set goals that are not confined by time, though we ourselves are.

These goals all lie beyond the horizon of any possible human achievement. But this does stop us from pursuing them. Indeed, we are drawn to them irresistibly. We not only *can* form ideals we are incapable of fully achieving. We *long* to achieve them. We cannot help wanting to do and be more than our mortal condition allows. Kant speaks of a "remarkable predisposition of our nature, noticeable to every human being, never to be capable of being satisfied by what is temporal."[10] Science, philosophy, literature, and art all spring from this unfulfillable longing.

Some of our goals, therefore, are ones we can neither avoid nor achieve. This dooms us to a special kind of disappointment. Among all the living things on earth, it is our distinctive fate to be disappointed in this peculiar and self-inflicted way.

Yet, amazingly, we are able to make progress even toward those goals that remain forever beyond reach—like knowing all there is to know about the world or loving our partners and friends as well as we long to do. We are not forever stuck in place, incapable of becoming wiser or more loving. This is a paradox of sorts. How is it possible to come closer to a goal that is always at the same impossible distance? Yet we not only accept the paradox. We live by it. It shapes our hopes and dreams. The possibility of progressive achievement in the shadow of sure disappointment defines the human condition. It is what makes us the strange but familiar beings we are.

Some find this hard to accept. They want to believe that

our deepest longings can be fulfilled. This is more than an understandable wish. It is the central teaching of the two otherwise remarkably different traditions of thought that in the West we associate with the names of Athens and Jerusalem.

Though antithetical in many ways, the Abrahamic religions and the great philosophical systems of pagan antiquity share one crucial characteristic. They assure their followers that our longing to reach God is not doomed to disappointment. This is the source of their lasting appeal. But it amounts to a rejection of the belief that our troubled condition is final. For an acceptance of the human condition, they substitute illusions of fulfillment.

Atheists like my mother and most of my friends are right to refuse the seductive promise of fulfillment, whatever form it takes. They correctly view it as antihumanistic. But they are wrong to conclude that humanists can do without any idea of God whatsoever. We need some idea of what Aristotle calls "the eternal and divine" to explain the meaning of those unattainable goals that give human life its peculiar drama, and to account for the fact that we can move closer to them without ever being able to overcome the gap completely.[11]

Given that we have such goals, and can approach but never reach them, what must we assume about the nature of reality in general in order to explain how this uniquely human experience is possible at all? How must we think about the world as a whole in order to account for our tragic but joyful place in it?

Following this line of inquiry brings us back to God, by an indirect route. It does not prove that God exists through arguments or experiences that transcend the limits of our time-bound condition. It neither invites nor requires us to put our humanity aside. What it shows is that the all-too-human experience of deep disappointment—of striving, progressing, yet always falling short—is intelligible only on the extravagant but compelling assumption that the world is inherently and infinitely divine.

This is the idea of God I defend in this book. It would be presumptuous to say I can prove it. But it is not just an article of faith either. So far as I can tell, my idea of God follows with all the weight of reason from a reflection on the meaning of the knowledge of death that my mother accepted as the fundamental fact of human life when she committed herself to the philosophy of Camus and Sartre. I do not see how a rational humanist can avoid it. Those who say, as many of my friends do, that we can account for the experiences that most poignantly define the human condition without *any* conception of God are as antihumanistic in one way as the traditional philosophies and theologies of fulfillment they reject are in another.

I am now twice the age my mother was when we sat on the steps of our home in California and she told me what she thought about God (nothing very flattering). I have come to the conclusion that she was at least partly wrong.

There *is* a God after disbelief. It is not the God my parents dismissed as a childish fantasy and my friends belittle. But it is a mistake to think we can dispense with the idea of God altogether. The fashionable belief that we can engenders a false picture of the human condition. It is as dishonest in its way as the religion my mother loathed is in another. We need the right idea of God to understand who we are. And we can find our way to it by reason alone, which my mother taught me is the only path to follow.

2

Endless Time

LAST AUGUST, I READ A letter in a local newspaper from an amateur astronomer. He said the best time to watch the annual Perseid meteor shower was four o'clock in the morning. I set my alarm to make sure I got up.

Recently, I renewed my gym membership and resolved to go four times a week. A year ago, my wife and I booked a flight to Venice. We planned to celebrate my birthday in an apartment on the Grand Canal.

Sometimes my plans go awry. My alarm failed to ring. My resolution to exercise faltered. My flight to Venice was canceled on account of a pandemic. Disappointment is a pervasive feature of human experience. (The last one was particularly sharp.)

Still, there is nothing about any of the goals I have mentioned, and countless others like them, that makes failure unavoidable. None is beyond reach. Failure may be common but it is contingent. It is a regrettable accident. Things might have turned out otherwise.

The same is true of many goals that cannot be reached even in a lifetime.

It often took more than a century to build the great cathedrals of Europe. Those who worked on them knew they would not live to see them finished. "The years of the [workman's] life passed away," Ruskin says, "before his task was accomplished; but generation succeeded generation with unwearied enthusiasm" until the building stood at last in its completed form.[1]

Sometimes the cathedral remained unbuilt. Political or other forces intervened. But the architect who designed the plans, and the first workman who lifted a hammer, conscious as they may have been of all the accidents that might spoil their work, were not embarking on a project impossible of completion. The end was attainable, in principle at least, subject to the usual risk of disappointment that haunts even our most modest ventures, like planning a picnic that may have to be canceled because of the weather.

In this respect, multigenerational projects of the kind of which the cathedral may serve as a type are no different from those a person can complete in a lifetime. Still, they have special importance to us. They respond to a distinctive and powerful human desire. They spring from the longing we all feel, at different times and in various ways, to be attached to something more lasting than ourselves.

I feel this, for example, when I contribute to the Nature Conservancy or read about NASA's plans to build a human colony on Mars. I feel it when I vote to appoint a young woman to the faculty of the Yale Law School, in the hope that she will still be teaching there when I am no longer alive.

These decisions and daydreams carry me, in imagination at least, beyond the horizon of my own life. I will not live to see them fulfilled. But in my mind's eye, I can picture the world still flourishing when I no longer am. This enlarges my sense of presence and purpose. It satisfies my longing to escape the confines of my life, in the only way I can.

The power that enables me to do this is already at work, in a humble and unnoticed way, when I make a plan today to arrange a picnic tomorrow. But it is most expansively and dramatically engaged when I look beyond the boundaries of my life as a whole and reflect on what the world will be like when I am no longer in it. The power that is active in this special kind of foresight is at once the most familiar and mysterious power we possess.

Like other animals, we live in time. We are born, exist for a while, and then die. But we alone *know* we will. This is our unique fate among living beings. No other has what Alexander Pope calls "the useless knowledge of its end."[2]

Death is for us not merely a fact—something that happens to us. It is an object of reflection. We may not think about it constantly, but the thought of death is never far away, and the ability to think about it is with us always, from the moment we emerge from the fog of infancy into the realm of conscious thought.

Other animals long to live, just as I do. They seek nourishment and avoid danger. The turtle I found in my garden last month pulled back into its shell when my shadow crossed its path. I watch sparrows dig for worms and chase hawks from their newborn chicks.

My dog, Maisie, is a wonderfully complex animal. She has refined desires and fears. She wants a warm spot close to the fire and the comfort of human companionship. She enjoys being rewarded for good behavior. Certain things terrify her— lightning and large dogs. She avoids pain and death, like the turtle and sparrows and me. But, so far as I can tell, Maisie is not anxious about dying. She never wonders or worries about it, as we do even in moments of relative safety. Nor do any other animals. They are all mortal too, but none of them knows it.

This knowledge is possible only because I can conceive of my life as filling a certain period of time that is not the whole of time but just a limited portion of it. This is an imperfect formulation. It suggests that *first* I contemplate some longer stretch of time *and then* think of myself as occupying a part of it, as if these were successive thoughts, one following the other. In truth they are the *same* thought, differently expressed. The knowledge of death *is* the awareness of a time longer than the period allotted to me: of a time "before" and "after" my life, however long I live.

Looking back, I can conceive of a time before I was born. I sometimes think about the American Revolution, for example. I've read books about what happened in Boston and Philadelphia. I follow the events they describe in my imagination, though it is impossible for me to have a direct experience of them.

The same is true looking forward. I've read about the collapse of the sun billions of years from now. Astrophysicists say this is certain to happen. I can picture it in my mind though I will not be alive to experience it; it is doubtful any human being will. Here, too, my imagination outstrips my experience. It does so in both directions, backward and forward. Were this not the case, I could not see my mortal limits. I would still *be* mortal, of course. But I wouldn't know it. The excess of imagination over experience and the knowledge of death are one and the same.[3]

The power that allows me to conceive a time longer than my life throws the brevity of my existence into painful relief. This may seem, in moments of despair, a liability I would avoid if I could. In *The Birth of Tragedy,* Nietzsche recounts the "old legend that king Midas for a long time hunted the wise Silenus, the companion of Dionysus." When he finally caught him, the king asked Silenus what is the best life for man. "Suffering creature, born for a day," Silenus replied, "the very best thing for you is totally unreachable: not to have been born, not to exist, to be nothing. The second best thing . . . is to die soon."[4]

Yet the same power that is the cause of our uniquely human suffering is also the source of the most distinctive freedom we know. It allows us to consider the world and ourselves from a vantage point other animals can never attain. It enables us to ask questions and pursue goals they cannot conceive.

What would have happened if the French had not intervened on our side in the American Revolution? Did Thomas Jefferson love Sally Hemings, and she him? Will the Yale Law School still exist in two hundred years? Will the planet be hotter then? Will my grandchildren grow up to be happy men and women and have happy children of their own?

I ask these questions and others like them from a point of view that is not confined by my mortality. My imaginative access to it does not make me any less mortal. But it transforms my experience of mortality in a basic way. It allows me to take an interest in what happened before I was born and will happen after I die.

The latter has special practical importance. That is because I can do something about it. I cannot change the course of the American Revolution. Perhaps I do not even care whether it succeeded or failed. My interest in the past may be entirely speculative. But knowing that the world will go on after my death, it is difficult if not impossible to be indifferent about its future course. I want the future to go one way rather than another, if only in the limited ways that are of personal concern

to me. Because I do, and because I have some small influence
in this regard, I have a reason to make plans that only my successors can complete.

The freedom that allows me to do this is one that human
beings alone possess. For the most part, I take it for granted.
What could be less remarkable than contributing to the Nature
Conservancy or setting money aside for my grandchildren?
Yet these actions and decisions are possible only because my
imagination carries me beyond my mortal existence to a world
I know will outlast me because I know there is more time than
however much of it I get to experience directly.

The knowledge that this is so is the origin of our deepest
anxieties. It is also the source of the freedom to plan beyond
the horizon of our all-too-brief lives. The latter offers a form
of fulfillment that only human beings ever experience. It is as
unique as the anxiety aroused by the correlative and inseparable knowledge of death. The first may not be a compensation
for the second. But it is the only reward we have.

So far as I can tell, other animals experience neither the
anxiety nor the reward. They are prisoners of their mortality
in a way we are not. We know we are going to die, and *because
of this* we can conceive of the world as something separate and
more lasting, ticking to the beat of a metronome that measures
our short span of time. With this thought, we are set up to
reach out to a world that will still exist when we no longer do,
and to plan for it now in ways that will affect it then.

Every goal that takes more than a lifetime to reach begins with this thought. It depends on the power that allows
us to think it. It starts with the knowledge of death. All our
multigenerational pursuits are conceived in the shadow of this
knowledge. They exhibit its liberating potential in a particularly striking way. But in truth every area of human experience,
no matter how trivial or "animalistic," is touched and trans-

formed by our awareness of death. The fantasies and anxieties that set our sex lives apart from those of other animals—to take just one example—are inseparable from the hopes and fears that our knowledge of mortality joins to the cosmic power of erotic attraction.[5]

This is all exceedingly familiar and yet, in a way, quite extraordinary. It reminds us that our experience of life, however accustomed we grow to it, springs from the uncanny power to see that we are living in time, as opposed to merely doing so.

This enables us to form plans whose fulfillment requires more time than our lives allow. Even more remarkably, it allows us to frame goals that cannot be reached in *any* period of time, however long.

Goals of the latter sort differ from cathedral building and projects like it. We are able, in principle at least, to fulfill even the grandest ambitions of this kind. It may take several lifetimes to do so. The risk of disappointment is commensurately great. But success is not out of the question.

A goal that cannot be reached in any period of time is by contrast absolutely unattainable. The disappointment that accompanies our effort to achieve it is assured. It is built into the nature of the goal itself. We can never hope to avoid such disappointment, even with all the luck in the world.

Let me give a few examples.

People have always been interested in the weather. Why does it rain some times and not others? Why are there periods of flood and drought? The questions are of practical importance. Pharaoh freed Joseph because he had a plan for dealing with a weather emergency. The current debate over climate change reminds us how important such plans can be.

Our ancestors developed methods for predicting the weather. They invented instruments to do this. Today, we can forecast the weather with astonishingly greater precision than ever before. But not perfectly. The idea of being able to predict with exactness what the weather will be like even five hours from now is a dream. That is because our knowledge of what causes the weather is still incomplete.

In 1825, Goethe wrote an essay titled "Toward a Theory of Weather." He remarked on the extraordinary advances made possible by the thermometer, barometer, and hygrometer (which measures relative humidity). Yet he noted that where the weather is concerned, "one thing is always permeated, accompanied, covered, or enveloped by another." How, Goethe asked, where "so many things work through one another," are we to "discover what governs and what serves, what leads the way and what follows?" He laconically concluded that this "creates great difficulty in any theoretical statement."[6]

We are in the same position today. The science of weather is advancing. It is much further along than when Goethe wrote, and even further than when Aristotle composed the first systematic treatise on the subject twenty-four hundred years ago.[7] But we will never run out of questions to ask about its causes and consequences. Answering some only prompts others. The age-old effort to understand the weather has no end. Its goal cannot be reached next year, or century, or in any finite period of time.

The same is true of the equally ancient attempt to define the principles of social justice and to implement them in a practically workable scheme.

Views about the proper definition of justice have differed since the beginning of serious reflection on the subject. The Greek Sophists claimed there is no universal standard of justice. Socrates insisted there is. Differences remain but the range of agreement is growing. Today nearly all of us agree that the slave and feudal societies of earlier times were unjust by comparison with the liberal democracies of our own. This represents an advance, like the discovery of atmospheric pressure. We are making progress in the pursuit of justice, too, though it is painfully slow, disturbingly incomplete, and beset by disagreements that do not lend themselves to scientific measurement and experimentation.

America is an example. Its history is one of fitful progress toward an inspiring but unattained goal. From the start, its promise of democratic self-government, tempered by the stability of a well-designed constitution, has been a beacon to the world. Yet America's ideals have been compromised from the beginning by the original injustice of slavery and its stubborn legacy. They have been frustrated by constitutional flaws of various kinds. Slavery has been abolished and many of these flaws repaired. Still, the stain of racial injustice remains. Some Americans wonder whether it can ever be erased.

This seems unduly pessimistic. Things are better today than they were a hundred years ago, in the era of Jim Crow. Viewed in a long perspective, America is moving forward. It is closer today than ever before to the realization of its ideals. Yet further challenges remain. They always will.

Martin Luther King famously said that he looked forward to the day when all Americans will be judged by "the content of their character," not "the color of their skin."[8] This is a noble ideal. It expresses an essential part of what we understand by the meaning of fairness. It has special resonance in the context of America's centuries-long reckoning with racial injustice.

But King's vision is utopian. To implement it fully would require that each citizen have some knowledge of every other's virtues and vices, in order to judge the worth of their character in the way that King imagines. This is not likely to happen any time soon. It is also incompatible with other values, like the autonomy of family life. We can reduce these tensions but never finally resolve them (nor should we wish to). King's ideal is admirable and approachable. But it is unattainable. We are drawn to it while recognizing that however close we come, a gap will still remain even if we had all the time in the world.

Our impassioned, fitful pursuit of love offers a third example. It repeats the same experience at a personal level.

Love is a work in progress. We often feel that we are either gaining ground or losing it—that our love is deepening, growing, becoming more expansive, or the opposite. The child who at last feels able to sympathize with the obsessive habits of an aging parent; the parent who has finally accepted, with a measure of affection, a child's unconventional career or unexpected sexual orientation; the lover who has come to see what before appeared a blemish in the beloved's body or soul as a beauty mark instead: all are growing in love, moving toward a more complete experience of it.

Yet love never reaches its goal. There is no human love, however rich and deep, that is not shadowed by the knowledge of its incompleteness. This is not the same as impermanence—the fact that even a perfect love, were such a thing attainable, is soon cut down by what Shakespeare calls time's "bending sickle."[9] It is the distance that exists at every moment between the love one feels, however great, and the greater love one might, time permitting. Time eventually runs out. But a gap still remains. No stretch of time is long enough to cross it.

Knowing all there is to know about the weather or any other aspect of the natural world; fashioning a perfectly just society; loving another person as well as one longs to do in one's most hopeful moments: these are what Kant calls "regulative" ideals. They guide our conduct *over* time toward goals we can never achieve *in* time. They inspire us to pursue what we cannot reach yet can approach more closely if we try.[10]

Goals of this sort are abstractions. We can conceive but never "see" them. Their meaning becomes clearer as we go, but the goals themselves cannot be captured in an imaginative portrait even of the blurriest kind, like that of the cathedral standing finished in the afternoon light, a hundred years from now. Still, this does not deprive them of their inspirational force or authority as a measure of progress, in our individual lives and across generations of time.

We set goals of this uniquely distant kind by an extension of the power that enables us to picture the world in the future, after we die. Our ability to do this rests on the knowledge that time goes on after our brief share of it has been exhausted. But knowing that time continues for a day, or a year, or a century after we die, we *also* know that it goes on for another day after *that,* and so on without end. The knowledge that time does not end with our death leads irresistibly to the thought that time is endless.

This too is an inexact formulation. It suggests that the second thought is a product of the first one. It could just as easily be put the other way around. It is only because we are *already* aware that time has no end, that we know that any discrete portion of it—my lifetime, say, or the next million years—has an end that will be followed by another period, of equal length, and so on forever. In one sense, the awareness that time is endless follows by extension from our knowledge that the world will still exist the day after we die. In another sense, it precedes this knowledge as its unstated condition.

The idea of endless time is one way of understanding what eternity means. No period of time is eternal. Each, however long, comes to an end. But time itself does not. Time is not an event *in* time. It is the eternal framework or foundation of everything that appears, exists, and then vanishes in the endless stream of time.

The idea of eternity in this sense gives us the "running room" we need to set goals that are by definition unattainable because they cannot be reached in any period of time, whatever its duration. It makes these goals conceivable. At the same time, it guarantees our disappointment. It ensures that there will always be a gap between the endless time we need to set such goals and whatever progress we make toward them in a lifetime or any number of lifetimes.

Our failure to close this gap is not an accident. It does not depend on contingent factors. Goals that we can reach before we die, and even those that we depend on our successors to achieve, do not present an insurmountable gap of this kind. The disappointments that accompany them are painful but not inevitable. They are *shallow* rather than *deep*.

Other animals experience shallow disappointments too. They have goals and often fail to reach them. The sparrow is disappointed when it misses the worm. So is my dog, Maisie, when her ball rolls under the bed. We alone set goals that can only be reached in an endless time that lies beyond the horizon of mortal experience, and know the special kind of disappointment these entail. Deep disappointment is our fate.[11] It is built into our peculiar constitution as beings who are able to conceive of endless time while confined by their mortality to a portion of it not much longer than the lives of sparrows and dogs.

I cannot picture endless time in the way I can the picnic I am planning for tomorrow or (more sketchily) my granddaughter's graduation from college. Still, it is a coherent and meaningful idea. But where "am I" when I have it? The answer seems obvious. I am right where I am now. It is Saturday morning, July 25, 2020, and I am writing and thinking about endless time—just as I am thinking about the picnic.

This is true, of course. But it is not the whole truth. That is more mysterious.

When I think about the picnic, I imagine one moment from the vantage point of another. But what about the idea of time without end? This is not the idea of a single moment, like the picnic, but of an endless series of such moments. It is the idea of time as a *whole,* of time *itself.* From what position or point of view do I frame such an extravagant notion?

To plan now for something later, I must be able to disengage myself from my immersion in the present. I have to be sufficiently detached from my current situation to take it as an object of reflection. This alone gives me the distance I need to deliberate about the causal relation between the preparations I make today and the picnic tomorrow.

Analogously, in order to form the idea of time itself—to take in all of time "at a glance"—I must be able to detach myself, in imagination at least, from time altogether. I cannot conceive the idea of endless time except from a point of view that is "above" or "beyond" or "outside" it.

The perspective I adopt when I form this idea is unconditioned by the familiar categories of "before," "after," "now," and "later" that shape my understanding of events as they occur in the stream of time. I need the idea of time without end—of eternity in one sense of the word—to explain the distinctively human experience of deep disappointment. Yet this very idea is one I can conceive only because I am able to assume a reflective stance to which none of these temporal categories applies.

This sounds exceedingly strange. But it describes a common experience. We know it from our schooldays as children. It is the experience of understanding a mathematical truth.

When I see why the area of the square erected on the hypotenuse of a right-angled triangle must be equal to the sum of the areas of the squares on the other two sides, I apprehend a timeless truth, however much time it has taken me to grasp it. Categories like "before" and "after" do not apply to the truth of what I know. Its truth does not "come to be." It will not "pass away." It does not grow or develop or die. It is immune to change because it does not belong to the order of time in which all change occurs.

We sometimes describe this experience by saying that the truths of mathematics are *eternal*. This is a familiar use of the word. But it does not mean "endless time" or "time everlasting." That is the idea of a series of moments, one after another, without end. Mathematical truths are eternal because they lie outside this series altogether.

Eternity therefore has two meanings. One (endless time) is defined in temporal terms. The other (timelessness) is characterized by the irrelevance of all terms of this kind. Mathematics has been the paradigm of eternity in this second sense since philosophers first began to wonder about permanence and change, or "being" and "becoming," as they were termed at the dawn of our philosophical tradition.[12]

These two ways of understanding the meaning of eternity are not only different. They are in a sense opposed. One is cast in the language of time; the other eschews it. Yet there is a relation between them. Anything that is eternal in the sense that it exists *outside* of time must, just for that reason, exist at every moment *in* time as well. The Pythagorean theorem is a timeless truth. Because it is, it must be true today, tomorrow, and always. Its timelessness guarantees its everlasting validity. It is eternal in the latter sense *because* it is eternal in the former.

This seems clear enough in the case of mathematics. But the realm of mathematical truth is not as unique as it seems. All the modern natural and social sciences rely on these same two ideas of eternity and presume a connection between them.

This is bound to seem implausible. We have grown used to the idea that mathematical truth is one thing and empirical truth another. Between them, many philosophers say, there is an unbridgeable chasm.[13] The belief that this is so hardened into a dogma long ago. Moreover, the idea of eternity seems far removed from the hardheaded work of scientific research. It seems preposterous to suggest that the ordinary labors of physicists, botanists, and economists depend on any idea of eternity—let alone two. Yet they do. We need the ideas of time-lessness and endless time, and the relation between them, to explain the most characteristic feature of every modern science— the one that makes it modern. This is its pursuit of a goal we can approach more closely over time but never reach, even with all the time in the world. In truth, we need the idea of eternity in both senses of the word to grasp the meaning of *every* pursuit of this kind. We need it to account for the uniquely human experience of deep disappointment, accompanied by the joy of growing power, that all such pursuits offer as their only reward—the search for justice and love as much as the quest for understanding. Modern science is only a particularly perspicuous example of a general phenomenon that more than any other defines the prospects and limits of the human condition.

Science is the collective name we give to a vast array of differ-ent disciplines. Some explore the structure of inanimate mat-ter. Others investigate the phenomenon of life. Still others study human behavior. Some scientists are interested mainly in what we call "theoretical" questions, while others engage in empiri-cal research, though the two are always intertwined to some degree. The diversity of subjects and methods is so great that one may reasonably wonder whether the single word *science* refers to anything meaningful at all.

Yet it captures something important. All these pursuits are today governed by a regulative ideal. Each seeks to discover and apply some set of timelessly valid laws or principles, through an endless process of conjecture, testing, and verification. The defining experience of modern science is that of progress toward a goal that always exceeds our grasp. Its spirit is the pathos of deep disappointment, punctuated by fitful advance.

This has not always been the case. The idea that scientists seek an unattainable end is a historical novelty. It is completely missing, for example, in the writings of Aristotle, the greatest philosopher of science in the ancient world.[14]

To understand the nature of the goal that so profoundly distinguishes our conception of science from his, it is useful to begin with the source from which both spring. All science, ancient and modern, is responsive to an elementary human desire. Aristotle calls it simply the "desire to know."[15]

Other animals are curious too. But only human beings desire to understand why things happen as they do. Only we explore the world in deliberately disciplined ways. At the start, our inquiries are limited and practical. Later they become more general and theoretical. Knowledge becomes an end in itself. Yet whatever their motive, or level of generality, all our efforts to understand the world are alike in one respect. They all proceed on the assumption that to explain anything, it must be brought under a *law* or *rule* of some kind.

Let me give an example from my own experience.

I spend a part of each year on a small island fifteen miles from the Rhode Island shore. It is a place of great natural beauty, abundant in fish. I love to fish and go whenever I can.

Suppose I want to know when I have the best chance of catching a striped bass. I try my luck at different times and places. I study the movements of the fish that I can see. I keep track of tides, seasons, and weather. Eventually I know enough to formulate a hypothesis. "Striped bass are hungriest on an incoming tide the day after a storm."

For my practical purposes, it is enough that the rule I have discovered describes a *correlation* between tides and weather, on the one hand, and the behavior of fish, on the other. I have no interest in understanding why this correlation exists—unless, of course, I am a scientist as well as a fisherman. In that case, I will want to know what *causes* fish to behave as they do. Suppose I pursue my research in a more disinterested way, now with the help of some laboratory equipment. I conclude that "fish are hungry after a storm *because* a rise in barometric pressure increases their production of endocrine, a hormone that stimulates appetite."

The difference between a correlation and a cause is relative, not absolute. Something is a cause only because it explains a correlation. Seen in this light, the relation between barometric pressure and endocrine level is a correlation too. To account for *it,* some further cause must be found. I continue my investigations and arrive at a deeper explanation. "A rise in barometric pressure causes an increase in endocrine by compressing the vagus nerve, which otherwise inhibits its production."

Aristotle thought the process of searching for causes cannot go on indefinitely. He was sure it must come to an end in a *final* cause, for whose explanation only a fool would ask. We no longer share Aristotle's belief in this regard. One of the hallmarks of modern science is the conviction that the process of searching for deeper explanations can and must continue forever.

This is reflected in the axiom that for a causal hypothesis to be of any value, it has to be *falsifiable.* It must be possible to show that what it proposes as a cause is at most a correlation that stands in need of explanation on the basis of some other, as-yet undetermined factor. A cause that needs no explanation is a tautology that explains nothing.[16]

Still, even if no causal explanation can ever be final, the *idea* of a cause, as distinct from a correlation, retains its commanding authority. It reminds us of the perpetual need for further research by underscoring the inadequacy of every explanation that stops at correlations alone. A correlation is merely a report. It says that one thing follows another or occurs in conjunction with it. But the observation that it does carries no implication that it must. The conjunction may be different the next time we look. We have no guarantee that it will be the same, unless there is a *necessary* connection between the events in question. The idea of a cause asserts the existence of a connection of this kind.

David Hume famously argued that we never possess a genuine knowledge of causes. All we ever know, he said, are the outward and observable correlations among events in the ever-changing world of sense experience. There is nothing necessary about these. The idea of a cause, Hume claimed, is that of a compulsory "inner" force we naively postulate but never experience. He thought the idea illusory—a fictive projection based on a loose and habitual way of speaking.[17] Many philosophers and scientists still accept Hume's view. But it is wrong in one crucial respect.

For a scientist, it is never enough merely to know that something *is* the case. She wants to know *why* it is the case. Her answers only lead to further questions. The process is endless. For it to come to an end, she would have to understand the cause of what she is studying. She would have to be able to explain why it cannot be other than it is. This is the inspiring if unattainable goal that guides her work.

Mathematical explanations provide an understanding of this kind. They fully satisfy our desire to know by establishing

the necessity of the connection between two different things—
the premise and conclusion of a geometrical proof, for example. Until a student sees this, he does not understand the explanation at all. When he does, he understands it completely.

The world of nature of course differs from that of mathematics. The first we encounter in experience, the second we
construct. We must look at nature and explore it to see what it
is and how it works. The discoveries of mathematics are built
by thought alone.

Aristotle recognized this distinction, as anyone must. But
he believed that if we study nature closely enough, we will
eventually understand why its laws cannot be other than they
are. We will see that they are as necessary as those of mathematics. This is precisely what Hume rejects. He insists that it
is a mistake to think we can ever discover the same sort of necessity in our investigations of the natural world as we rightly
expect in mathematical ones.

There is an irony in this. Modern science is heavily dependent on the techniques of mathematics. Aristotle makes
virtually no use of them. Hume's followers applaud the use of
these techniques but at the same time insist that the idea of a
cause is a metaphysical illusion that illicitly imports into the
work of scientific research a concept of necessity that belongs
to mathematics alone.

Their view captures an important truth. Our finite powers limit us to observing the "outward" relations among events.
Their real "inner" cause remains forever inaccessible. Yet at the
same time, we are never content with the observation of correlations alone. Our desire to know why things happen as they
do cannot be satisfied in full until every explanation but one
has been ruled out. All other explanations must be shown to
be not merely improbable but strictly inconceivable.

This is what the idea of a cause purports to do. It expresses a mathematical ideal. The ideal continues to guide the work of science today, as it did Aristotle's reflections on the goal of scientific research, with the crucial difference that he thought the goal attainable and we do not.

This guarantees that disappointment is built into the modern sciences of nature and society. But the shortfall between achievement and goal, which we now take for granted, does not mean that the goal itself has lost its meaning. If it had, the perseverance of our desire to know in the face of sure defeat would make no sense at all.

Our perseverance is justified by the fact of progress, even if the final end remains as distant as before. We are gaining ground in our understanding of the world in the many, varied branches of research that are inspired by the endless search for causal explanations. Galileo had a sounder view of motion than his Aristotelian rivals. Newton advanced beyond Galileo and Einstein beyond Newton. Quantum mechanics represents a still further advance. Darwin's theory of evolution explains the "tree of life" in ways unimaginable two hundred years ago. The same is true in economics. Its predictions are notoriously imprecise. But the modern science of economics enables us to understand production and exchange in ways that were unthinkable before Adam Smith.

There is something paradoxical about this. How can we make progress toward an unreachable goal? But the practitioners of modern science are not deterred by the paradox. They accept it without a blush, as do the rest of us who happily consume the fruits of their research without stopping to wonder how a process can be progressive and interminable at once.

The paradox cannot be dissolved. But it can be understood. We need the idea of eternity in both senses of the word to understand it.

A cause purports to explain its effect. The relation between them is conceived in temporal terms. An effect *follows* its cause or occurs *simultaneously* with it. The ball moves across the table *after* having been struck by the cue; the gravitational pull of the moon causes a *concurrent* rise and fall in the tides. Causal explanations are always temporally "inflected." They employ the "tensed" terms we use to describe the position in time of one event vis-à-vis another ("before," "after," "simultaneously").

Mathematics is different. The premises of a proof explain the conclusion, just as the impact of the cue explains the movement of the ball, and the mass of the moon the motion of the tides. But the connection between premises and conclusion is not a temporal one. It may take time to understand. But the relation that explains why the second follows from the first is not one of "before" and "after" in a temporal sense. Nor is it one of temporal simultaneity either. The conclusion would follow from the premises even if it occurred at a different moment in time. Mathematical explanations are true, when they are, independently of time. This is what distinguishes them from causal explanations and gives them a necessity the latter can never possess.

Aristotle recognized the difference between these two sorts of explanation. But he believed that in one sense it can be overcome. If we observe nature carefully, he says, we are able to grasp the principles that explain the motions of everything in it. With further study, we can understand the ultimate cause of these principles themselves. At the pinnacle of our investigations, we see why this final cause cannot be other than it is. When we do, we possess a form of knowledge as timeless as that of a mathematician. We not only see *that* the processes of nature occur in a regular and intelligible way, but also know *why* they *must*. We understand that the laws of nature are eternal in both senses of the word, just like the laws of mathematics.

Today this seems a laughable ambition. But what makes it so implausible is not the goal itself. The goal is one we share. What seems ridiculous is Aristotle's confident belief that the goal can be reached by a serious student of nature in a single lifetime of study.

Modern science rests on the assumption that the gap between what we know about the world and what we long to know cannot be closed in any number of lifetimes. Yet the aim of those engaged in the interminable work of scientific research remains what it was for Aristotle. Like him, they seek to explain what happens in the world in terms of the relation of cause and effect, and to account for these temporal relations on the basis of laws that apply always and everywhere because their validity is unconditioned by time.

The process is endless. It begins with the observation that two events are correlated. We want to explain why. We suggest that one event does not merely follow from or occur simultaneously with the other but is caused by it. Every such proposal is tentative and controversial. It requires further validation. This takes place over time—indeed, an endless time. There will always be alternative hypotheses to consider and disconfirm. But as we do, our understanding of causes becomes clearer and more confident. More of the world becomes intelligible to us. We see that things do not just happen in a temporal order. We see that their relations are governed by laws whose operation is as certain as those of mathematics, which in a strict sense never "happen," because they exist outside of time altogether.

Could we reach the end of this pursuit, we would see that there are no mere correlations; that everything is caused; that what happens in time happens with the necessity of a mathematical proof; that every provisional empirical claim about the temporal regularities we observe in the natural world is just a way station on the road to a fully elaborated system of conceptual truths that is no more dependent on time than the Pythagorean theorem or any other mathematical proposition. Could we reach our goal, we would have closed the gap between time and eternity.

This sounds outlandish. Who in his or her right mind seeks something so extravagant? A few philosophers, perhaps, but surely not the level-headed men and women engaged in the workaday business of scientific research. Yet this is exactly what even the most down-to-earth scientist is striving to do.

The only really outlandish thought is that the goal can ever be reached. We know that even with all the progress in the world, we are bound to be disappointed. The gap between time and eternity is one we long to close but never can.

Aristotle recognized the longing. He thought it inconceivable that we could have such a longing and be unable to fulfill it. David Hume gave up on the longing itself. With a kind of genteel bemusement, he consigned it to the museum of human follies. The goal that inspires the work of modern science affirms the longing (contra Hume) and accepts the impossibility of its fulfillment (contra Aristotle). It guides the search for eternal truths that we can always better but never fully understand, because doing so would require an eternity of time.

In this sense, modern science does not dissolve the idea of eternity as it may sometimes seem to do, on account of its unsettling discoveries that what once appeared to lie beyond time's reach is as transient as everything else (the earth, the stars, the species of plants and animals, including humankind). Nor does it undermine the belief that our desire to understand the world reflects our longing to be connected to eternity, insofar as we are able.

What modern science challenges is the conviction that we can ever satisfy this longing. Some still think we can. They continue to believe in the reality of an afterlife or some other form of eternal existence, and in our ability to reach it. Their faith is countercultural. Its prospects for survival are doubtful. It runs against the current of modern life, which is shaped at every level, personal and public, by the experience and expectations of modern science. But the loss of faith in our ability to complete the voyage to eternity does not render the goal incoherent or destroy our desire to be under way.

This loss is one important aspect of the phenomenon of disenchantment. It is an expression of disbelief. Modern science speeds it along. But disenchantment does not nullify the aim of scientific research, which remains what it has always been: to find the eternal in time, though we now know we never shall. The truth is the opposite. Disenchantment is essential to the meaning of science, as we understand it today, for could we magically be restored to an enchanted world again, the idea of endless, progressive striving would make no sense at all.

Pursuits of this uniquely human kind, with their mix of disappointment and joy, are what remain of the idea of eternity and our desire to reach it once the confidence that we can is gone. They emerge into conscious light only when the work of disenchantment is done.

But disenchantment is not the origin of the ideals that guide these pursuits. That lies in the knowledge of death that is a permanent fixture of the human condition. Through a simple but irresistible extension of the power this knowledge involves, we are led to set goals that we can neither avoid nor fully achieve, yet are able to approach, in an endless time, to an ever-increasing degree. The work of modern science exemplifies this defining human experience in an especially striking way.

The search for social justice does so too, if more ambiguously.

The setbacks here are more frequent and discouraging than in the field of scientific research. Progress is more tentative and controversial. Still, there is a parallel between the two.

The pursuit of social justice seeks principles that will be rationally defensible to every human being, regardless of his or her situation. It aims to discover and defend timeless moral and political truths—to settle the question of justice from what John Rawls calls the perspective of "eternity."[18] The modern idea of human rights is an example.

If the search for these truths is progressive, but endless, as it appears to be, then we may with some justification describe the pursuit of social justice, like that of scientific understanding, as an eternal undertaking, too (in one sense of the word), whose goal is the discovery of eternal laws (in the second sense). The analogy is inexact. But it suggests how our most distinctively human goals retain their basic form from one endeavor to another and reflect the experience of deep disappointment that is our burden and privilege alone.

The modern understanding of love shows something similar.

Here the comparison with science is bound to seem even more remote. Love stands at the opposite end of human experience. It takes a high degree of specialized training to participate in any program of scientific research. By contrast, we are all engaged in the "work" of love. Different people succeed to different degrees, but the knowledge of how to succeed, if it exists at all, is not the privileged possession of an educated few. Love is also personal in a way that science is not. A woman who devotes her life to science knows that others will continue her work after she dies. She cannot count on anyone else to carry on her search for love when she is gone.

Yet different as they are, the modern forms of love and science have something important in common. Each aims at a goal that requires an endless time to reach. The idea of endless time is born with our knowledge of death and accompanied by the special kind of disappointment that every goal that depends on this idea inevitably brings. The approachable but unattainable ideal of love that defines our modern understanding of it fits this general pattern. It reveals the pathos of the human condition with a clarity no earlier ideal of love did. In this respect, it resembles the ideal of modern science, which is distinguished from its ancient predecessors in precisely the same way. The remoteness of love from science makes the resemblance all the more striking.

Plato was the first to offer a theory about the role of love in human life. He presents it in a dialogue called the *Symposium*. It is the best-loved of all his works. It has delighted centuries of readers and inspired countless imitations. You do not need to be a philosopher to understand or enjoy it. I read an extract at my daughter's wedding.[19]

The *Symposium* tells the story of a dinner party that Socrates attended, many years before the dramatic date of the dialogue itself, at the home of his friend Agathon to celebrate Agathon's victory in the dramatic festival at Athens that year. The guests have all been drinking hard for several days. They agree to a more sober celebration and settle on the idea of offering a round of speeches in praise of love.

Socrates is the sixth to speak. When it comes his turn, Socrates disclaims any original understanding of love. He says that everything he knows about it he learned from a wise woman named Diotima.

The gist of Diotima's account is that human love, in all its diverse forms, is always the love of the very same thing. It is always and only the love of eternity. This is the true object of every species of human love, base or noble. Its other features are a distraction or disguise.

All love, Diotima says, arises from a lack. It is the experience of a deficiency—of missing something and yearning to possess it in order to fill a void. A being that lacked nothing would love nothing, unless the longing for its own continued completeness could be called a kind of love.

Even the pair of mallard ducks I watched this spring, paddling in my pond, always together, huddled against the wind and rain, were working to fill a void. They needed each other to be complete—to make a nest and raise the next generation of ducks. Observing them, I was tempted to say they loved one another, in an extended sense of the term. But human love is different. It is characterized by a reflective knowledge of a deficiency the ducks share but do not see. It arises from the anxious awareness of our mortality.

This is our greatest shortcoming. It is the source of all our woes. We *know*, in a way that other animals do not, that the cause of all our troubles is our lack of permanence and vulnerability to change. What we most desire, therefore, is the one thing that will remedy this deficiency: a connection to or association with something that lasts forever. This is the motive, Diotima says, of all human love, from the elevated sort represented by philosophy to the most carnal variety, which, to the extent it is human at all, is animated by the same conscious longing for eternity that distinguishes human love from that of my ducks.

Diotima's claim that all love is of the eternal hardly fits the facts of experience. When one person loves another, eternity is generally the farthest thing from his mind. He wants to spend more time with his beloved, but knows the hours are fleeting. He knows that death marks the limit of their time together. He is aware that passions cool, that the one he loves today may not be the one he loves tomorrow. And the things he loves in the one he does will all dim and disappear: the lustrous hair that one day will be gray, the laughing eyes that will lose their light, the wit that will decline into the senility of age. The lover's passion, while it lasts, is for changeable things whose evanescence is the source of their appeal, or at least inseparable from it. He is not thinking about eternity at all—only tomorrow.

That this is what most love is like, Diotima concedes. But it is bound, she says, to end in disappointment.

Lovers always want more than their partners can provide. The moments they spend together are never as fulfilling as they wish, and there are never enough of them. Love is the most powerful passion we feel. But there is bound to be a gap between desire and fulfillment, so long as we give our love to those qualities of body and mind whose transience guarantees that they must sooner or later fail to satisfy the love they aroused.

There is a remedy for this disappointment. It pulls the sting of love once and for all. Who, knowing what the remedy is, would not avail herself of it? Diotima assumes we all want relief. The problem is not a lack of desire but ignorance about the proper cure.

The cure, she says, is to train ourselves to look through the superficial appearances of beauty we see in the beloved's smile and noble bearing, and to view these as the short-lived signs of what lies beyond the destructive power of time. We must habituate ourselves to see all mortal beauties as the multitudinous, shifting expressions of one unchanging and eternal Beauty. And then we need to shift our affection from the one to the other. We must learn to love Beauty in itself and for its own sake, apart from its countless, fugitive manifestations. This is the only path to relief.

Diotima knows it is not an easy path to follow. It runs against the grain of human feeling. But only when the passion of love has been redirected in this way, from mortal objects to an immortal one, does the threat of disappointment recede and finally vanish.

The process is not completed all at once. It proceeds in stages. Most never get beyond their love of other human beings, with their blemished, dying looks. A few rare souls go on to the love of something worthier. They devote themselves to their cities, which have no predetermined life span. They spend their time making just and beautiful laws; after they die, their names live on in civic memory. But laws are eventually corrupted; cities fall; fame attenuates and then disappears. Even the noblest politician loves what is fraught with disappointment. To escape it, he must set his sights still higher.

Only the philosopher whose eye for eternity has been sharpened through years of study at last loves what can never disappoint him. The longing for what alone can repair the deficiency of our mortal condition is finally and fully satisfied in the philosopher's love of what Plato calls the "Forms": the eternal principles of order that shape, direct, and generate the entire world of mutable things, of youthful lovers and teeming cities, and everything else that belongs to the "realm of sights and sounds." Others love what the philosopher does, but obscurely, mistakenly, under illusions of one kind or another. Only he holds, in his mind, the eternity that every human being longs to possess, mostly in ignorant and self-defeating ways. The philosopher is the only successful lover.

Diotima describes the lover's progress from human to civic to philosophical objects as a kind of ladder. Climbing it is emancipatory. It liberates those who do from the self-deluding forms of love that keep most people imprisoned in a kind of dreamlike stupor. It rewards the rare spirit who reaches the top with an unassailable grasp of what he or she (like every human being) has been striving to reach all along.

A few philosophers complete the journey in this life. While they live, they are distracted, like the rest of us, by physical need and the noisy demands of others. They experience the perfect fulfillment of love, but only in the interval between these distractions. Freed from the body after death, they enjoy forever the possession of the eternal truths they taste briefly before they die. Others never reach the goal, on either side of the grave. Their love is unrequited. But the goal is not beyond our grasp. That we could have a passion so deep and urgent and be permanently prevented from fulfilling it is inconceivable to Plato. The very idea is absurd. Its rejection is the cornerstone of his theory of love, which he puts in the mouth of his teacher, who puts it in the mouth of his own.

Few ever climb Diotima's ladder of love. Today, even the ambition seems uninviting. That is because we live in a democratic age. We believe in the moral and political equality of all human beings. Nothing is more democratic than love. It is something we all want. Success and failure are distributed equally. Diotima's view of love is by contrast fiercely aristocratic. Success in loving, she says, is a function of knowledge, and true knowledge is the possession of philosophers only. Her view is out of touch with the democratic spirit of our times.

For the past two thousand years, every branch of Western culture has been inspired by a very different ideal of love, one more in tune with democratic values. The philosophy, art, and literature of the West have all matured under the influence of the Christian ideal of love, which is radically different from Diotima's.[20]

This ideal is no mere byproduct or accidental offshoot of the teachings of the Christian religion. Christianity is at its heart a religion of love. It puts God's love for man at the center of its story of salvation. We are fallen creatures, stained by sin, but will be saved through God's inconceivably great love for us, if only we love God in return.

Christianity affirms a view of human love, too—of the love that exists among human beings, as distinct from our love of God. Many still accept this view. Indeed, many who no longer believe in the God of the Christian religion still think of human love according to a pattern that Christian beliefs fixed long ago.

The most striking thing about the Christian ideal of love is the value it assigns to individuals.

The Platonic ideal does just the opposite. It denigrates the individuality of the human beings we love, along with that of everything else in the world. The qualities that make one person different from every other belong to the world of appearances. They come and go in the blink of an eye. The sound of the beloved's voice, her way of telling a joke, her personal history and physical habits: none of these has any value in itself because none has even the slightest share in eternity. They are unworthy of our affection.

Those who focus on such things are deluded in love. They need to readjust their sights. They must train themselves to see the beloved as an instance or example of Beauty itself, which has no individual characteristics at all. In Plato's view, true love is always of what is general or abstract. Individuality is a dangerous mirage.

The Christian ideal of love turns this on its head. It celebrates individuality. It invites us to love other human beings *on account* of the qualities that make them the unique men and women they are—*not despite* these qualities, as Diotima says we should.

This is reflected, most poignantly, in the value the Christian religion assigns to the individuality of the one who died on the Cross so that the rest of us might live. Christ is not an idea. He is not an abstraction. He is a flesh-and-blood, suffering individual. Were he not, his sacrifice would be meaningless. It would not be a sacrifice at all. How Christ can be an individual in this excruciatingly real way, and at the same time the eternal Son of God, is the central mystery of the Christian religion.[21]

The value that Christianity assigns to the individuality of every human being is ultimately traceable to the doctrine of divine creation. Like Judaism before it and Islam after, Christianity teaches its followers that the world was created from nothing by an omnipotent God. This means that everything in the world is God's creation. The general laws that direct the overall operation of things are his invention. But so are the individual quirks that distinguish each creature from every other. Your individuality and mine display God's creativity in uniquely distinctive ways. Each exhibits his eternal wisdom and power from a singular point of view.

We love God by loving what we can see of him in the world he has created. If we love another human being for the qualities that distinguish her from everyone else, this is part of what loving God means. Our love of Christ is different, of course. We do not love Christ as one of God's creatures. He is an aspect of God himself—the visible one we can see. Other human beings are not divine in the same sense. But they are connected to God and reveal his eternal being, down to the smallest details of their bodies and personalities. When I love another man or woman, I do not need to look through these details to see the face of God. He is there, as Paul Simon says, in "the way she brushed her hair from her forehead."[22]

We still understand and admire this sentiment today. It is the result of the immense investment of value in the individuality of every human being that the doctrine of creation begets—even for those who no longer accept the doctrine itself.

There is, however, another side to the Christian conception of love—one that brings it closer to the Platonic view, from which it is otherwise so distant.

If God is visible in the special looks of the beloved, it is a terrible mistake, a sin really, to confuse the two. We must strive to keep them apart. God may create everything in the world, the individuality of my beloved included. But God is not *in* the world or *of* it. He transcends the world altogether.

When I love the one I do for her own sake, as a beauty in her own right, and not as a creature of God, to whom her existence and all that it includes is due, I ignore the chasm that separates God from the world. This is the mark of all "worldly" or carnal love. It is as grave an error for a Christian as the confusion of the world of sights and sounds with the eternal realm of Forms is for Plato—worse, in fact, because for Plato the error is one of understanding, whereas for a Christian it is a criminal act of disobedience.

So long as we are alive, we are subject to the temptations of carnal love. We must struggle to resist them. Those who succeed will be rewarded with the fulfillment of their longing for love. It will not come in this life (as Plato thought it can), but in heaven, after we die. There, God's obedient children will be reunited with their creator, and with the other human beings they have loved during their pilgrimage on earth. Somehow, though we cannot say how, they will share an eternal vision of

God in which their love for him is seamlessly fused with that of all the particular people whose individual traits they found so beautiful, for a time, while they walked from birth to death.[23]

The second will not be burned off for the sake of the first, as Plato maintains, but merged with it in a fashion we cannot comprehend. Still, every faithful Christian knows it shall come to pass. He knows that his longing for love will be fully and finally requited, in an eternal joy immune to the storms of time. It is as inconceivable to him that he should be forever barred from reaching his goal as it is to Plato.

Dante's *Commedia* is the supreme literary expression of this ideal of love, as the *Symposium* is of Plato's. These two ideals are profoundly different. Yet they share a crucial premise. Both rest on the belief that all human love is ultimately of the eternal and reflect the same confidence that our longing for eternity can and will be fulfilled.

The ruling ideal of love today differs from these other two. I shall call it the "romantic" ideal of love. It molds the way we think and talk about love and the feelings of transport, hope, and loneliness that go with it. It suffuses our contemporary understanding of every aspect of this basic human longing and inspires its representation in works of art that run the gamut from Henry James's *The Golden Bowl* to Willie Nelson's "You Were Always on My Mind."

The romantic ideal of love sets a goal we cannot reach, yet, with commitment and luck, are able to approach to an increasing degree. Like every ideal of this kind, it directs us in time toward an end that no amount of time is sufficient to allow us to achieve. Its meaning is inseparable from the idea of eternity in the first sense of the word and perhaps the second too (though this is more obscure).[24]

The word *romantic* suggests a special kind of intimacy—

the intensely passionate sort that generally involves sex. But this is only a particularly striking example of a more general phenomenon. In broad terms, the romantic ideal also shapes our view of the relation between friends, and even between parents and children. Through a familiar extension, it applies to the relation between citizens and nations as well. Romantic nationalism is as distinctively modern a form of love as the personal kind depicted in novels.[25]

The romantic ideal is a way of viewing the meaning of love in all its various guises. The differences among these matter, just as those among the branches of science do. Biology is not physics, and both differ from economics. The same is true of the relations between lovers, friends, and family members. These have distinct purposes and values as well. But the whole of modern love bears the imprint of a single, overarching ideal, just as modern science does.

The romantic ideal of love is the descendant of the Christian ideal. Like the latter, it assigns immense importance to the individuality of the human being one loves. The beloved may be a lover in the ordinary sense of the word; or a child or friend; even, by extension, a nation. The first involves sex; the others do not. In the last, the beloved is an entire community defined by a shared culture and history. But what one loves, in each case, is not some general excellence or virtue that the beloved happens to display. That is Diotima's view. If she were right, then the lover who is asked why he loves the one he does could answer by providing a list of positive attributes ("he is beautiful, smart, kind, clever, and modest"). That would be enough. But romantic love, in all its hues and shapes, rests on the belief that the deepest, truest love begins only where lists of this kind end.

The romantic lover loves the one she does (partner, child, friend, or nation) *because* the beloved is unique in all the world.

This is what distinguishes romance from lust, the love of a son or daughter from the perpetuation of one's genes, and patriotism from humanitarianism. The essence of romantic love is the conviction that the beloved is beautiful, worthy, and deserving of sacrificial concern *on account of* the concatenation of traits that set him or her apart from everyone else.

The belief that individuality matters is a defining feature of the Christian conception of love as well. But for an orthodox Christian, the uniqueness of the beloved has no value *in itself.* Its value comes from God. It is entirely derivative. To attribute an inherent worth to the looks, the voice, the feelings, the character, or the history of the beloved is a species of *idolatry.*

The romantic ideal of love reverses this judgment. It celebrates what the Christian ideal denigrates. It values the love of individuality *for its own sake,* as something precious *in its own right.* It detaches the value and meaning of worldly love from its prospective consummation in an otherworldly heaven. The romantic ideal is what remains of the Christian ideal of love in an age of disenchantment.

The Christian ideal shifts the final target of love from its immediate human object to God. The Platonic conception of love does something similar. In each case, the real object of the love we feel for other human beings lies elsewhere. It is a mistake (or sin) to love them in their own right, as the individuals they are. Those who do are fools, Diotima says. They are blinded by appearances. From a Christian point of view, they are sinners who confuse the human image of God with its divine original. The romantic lover loves directly what these other ideals say we ought to love only as the expression of something else. All forms of love—spousal, parental, friendly, and civic— reflect this humanistic judgment, insofar as they come under the dominance of the romantic ideal.

Every branch of love has a distinctive code of loyalty. Parents who love their children feel a special obligation to feed and educate them and make sure they grow into responsible adults. Friends are bound by ties of loyalty too. Up to a point, they give each other's needs and interests special weight. Patriots are loyal to their country in a way they are to no other. Amorous partners, married or not, often feel bound by a particularly rigorous code of loyalty that demands they keep their relation exclusive (the sexual part, at least, and sometimes the emotional part, too).

Each sort of loyalty entails certain duties. A failure to meet them is a failure of love. The father who treats his own children exactly as he does those of others is not a loving parent.[26] The woman who shows no greater desire to be with her friend than anyone else is hardly a friend at all. The lover who cheats and the adulterous spouse are dramatically disloyal. The love they profess is less than it seems. It may be entirely fraudulent.

There is nothing particularly "romantic" about any of this. Loyalty and disloyalty are age-old phenomena. They exist wherever there are parents, friends, and sexual partners, whatever the ruling ideal of love may be.

When it is that of romantic love, however, loyalty acquires a further meaning in all these different relationships. In addition to everything else, it means taking an interest in the individuality of the people we love, making an effort to see and appreciate their unique qualities, and helping bring these to rewarding expression.

On this view, part of what it means to be a loyal parent is encouraging one's children to discover their special passions, while developing the general skills they need to pursue them. It means embracing the individuals they become, even when their values carry them far from home. When I was nineteen and told my parents that I wanted to quit college and become a political organizer, they swallowed hard but accepted the decision and stood by me in the difficult time that followed. It was an act of parental love.

In a similar way, part of what it means to be a loyal partner, on the romantic view of love, is the willingness to yield, professionally, emotionally, and financially, so that one's lover or spouse can follow the plan she feels she must to become the person she longs to be, and then to support her plan, which may be tentative and obscure, in a spirit of collaborative warmth. We recognize when this happens—and more often, perhaps, when it doesn't. The pleasure and sadness this stirs is romantic.

In the film *Jerry Maguire,* a successful sports agent has a crisis of conscience. He makes a passionate speech to his firm about the importance of putting the welfare of clients before money. He is cheered and then fired.

When Jerry walks out of the office, he asks, "Who's coming with me?" Only Dorothy (an accountant he's met but once) follows him. Jerry's rapacious fiancée dumps him instead. But Dorothy believes in his plan. She believes in Jerry and wants him to be the man he longs to be. She supports him with tenderness and toughness, in equal measure.

In the end it all works out. Jerry's life is going in the right direction. Having neglected Dorothy and spurned her love, he at last sees how rare it is. He comes back to ask for her forgiveness and pledge his love in return. She tells him everything is all right. "You had me at hello," she says. It is one of the great romantic lines in film. We know exactly what she means and know that the two of them (and her little boy) will be together for the rest of their lives.[27]

None of this is easy. We fail more often than succeed. The romantic ideal is an aspirational goal that measures our actions and feelings by how close we come to meeting it. Other ideals of love do this too. But the romantic ideal includes an element the Christian and Platonic ideals do not. It defines success, in part at least, by our capacity to promote the individuality of those we love, as something of value in itself.

In every branch of human love touched by this ideal, the meaning of loyalty is adjusted to include this novel goal. It does not displace the other elements of loyalty. But it supplements them, as a capstone of sorts. To want others to be the best version of the individuals they are, and to support them in the venture, becomes, under the authority of the romantic ideal, the highest expression of human love.

This new goal creates a special challenge.

We can know many things about another person. We can identify many of his or her habits and traits. We can form a reasonably good idea of the person's wishes, regrets, and desires. Those who are sexually intimate are likely to know a good bit about each other's bodies and passions (though often less than they think). All this adds up to a more or less reliable picture of the person—of who he or she *is*. The picture fills in and becomes more consistent over time.

But no one's individuality is every fully captured by a picture of this kind. It is at best a summary or outline, subject to further refinement and sometimes wholesale revision. We are constantly being surprised by what other people do, even those we thought we knew extremely well. The surprise is often greatest in these cases. The more we think we know about a person, the more striking any unexpected sentiment, action, or judgment is likely to be.

A person's individuality is an inexhaustible source of innovation and surprise. It is a bottomless well. We can never fathom it completely.

This does not mean that individuality is completely sto-
chastic. A person does not one day mysteriously become someone wholly different for no reason at all, like Gregor Samsa in
Kafka's story, who wakes up to find himself transformed into a
bug.[28] Individuality unfolds in ways that have a measure of dis-
cernible order. Even the most disjointed lives are continuous
to a degree. That is why we can tell a story about them. But no
biography, however complete, ever fully captures the uniqueness of the human being whose life displays, but cannot de-
plete, the source from which it springs. There is always more
to discover about every human being than the most attentive
observer knows, or the most skilled biographer can convey.

The implications for the romantic ideal of love are mo-
mentous.

The ideal prompts us to love those we do as the individuals they are. It assumes their individuality is precious for its
own sake. But how can we live up to this ideal if the uniqueness of the people we love, though it comes more clearly into
view the longer our relationships last, always escapes full understanding? And if we can never completely *know* it, how can
we possibly *love* it?

Given our finite powers of cognition and feeling, the romantic ideal of love asks more than we can ever deliver. It is
an unattainable ideal, in contrast to the Platonic and Christian
conceptions of love, which assume a harmony or equilibrium
between striving and attainment.

Yet we all believe that it is possible to make progress—to
be better lovers than we are. The belief is indefeasible, however
often we are blocked or set back in the adventure of love. God
knows how often that is! But the prospect of progress is as real
a feature of love in every relationship conditioned by the romantic ideal as the inevitability of falling short in the end.

To reach our goal, we would need an endless time, as we

do in science. There, at least, we can imagine others continuing on our behalf after we are dead. The gap between the endless time we need to be the lovers we long to be, and the limited time we have to become them, is more painfully obvious here than in any other human experience.

This is not just the pain of being unable to spend one more day with the person we love. There is a further anguish beyond this. It comes from the knowledge that the relationship has not yet been exhausted; that there is always room to grow; that with more time, greater love is possible. There is no moment of completion in love—no moment at which one can say, as Faust thinks he wants to be able to say, "Stay, you are so beautiful."[29] The longing to be able to say this and the impossibility of ever doing so define the pathos of romantic love.

That we feel this pathos, punctuated by the exhilaration of loving and being loved a little better than before, when from time to time we do, and are, is possible only because among all the time-bound beings in the world, we alone possess the idea of endless time, or eternity in the first sense of the word. Romantic love is what the idea of eternity becomes when the longing to reach it remains but our incapacity to do so is accepted as an inescapable fate. Like modern science, it reflects the aspiring, troubled, intermittently joyful state that we inhabit as beings who, though confined to a portion of time, are able to think their way beyond it.

Scientists today are steered by an ideal that relies on the idea of eternity in two senses of the word. Their goal is the discovery of necessary truths unconditioned by time. They need an endless time to find them.

Love is different. Romantic lovers long to know and embrace the individuality of those they love. This is an endless adventure, too. But their goal is not the discovery of something that exists by necessity. They are not striving to find anything timeless.

Indeed, the opposite seems to be true. What can be more accidental than making a friend or finding a lover? The chances of meeting *just this one* are unimaginably small. That the two of us, out of all the people in the world, should have crossed paths and become friends or lovers is a bit of incredible luck.

The same is true of parents and children. It is an accident that I was born to the parents I was, and just as accidental that I have the children I do—two sons and two daughters, rather than fewer children, or more, or none at all, or children with different personalities. Love is a kingdom of accidents. The idea that these can somehow be converted into necessities, in the way scientists strive to do, seems preposterous.

But this is not quite the whole story. Romantic love has another, more mysterious side.

The longer love lasts, the more difficult it becomes for friends, partners, parents, and children to imagine loving anyone else in the same way. The harder it becomes to think of life without them. Beyond a certain point, the whole of one's life is so intimately bound up with these particular human beings that the experience and meaning of life itself is inseparable from them. This is sometimes expressed by saying that these relationships are the only imaginable ones; that life is inconceivable without them; that it is no accident to have found the friend one has, or fallen in love, but a kind of destiny instead.

In thinking about our own existence, we are often struck by two contrary thoughts. One is that nothing could be more accidental. It is depressingly easy to imagine the world without me. The other is that my nonexistence is absolutely inconceivable. The world needs me to be complete. How could it get along in my absence?

Something similar is true of our relationships with the

particular people we love. What could be more accidental? And yet what is more difficult to imagine than these relationships not existing, or others taking their place?

Those who are most deeply in love have both of these thoughts or feelings at once. The experience of living with them, and the tension between them, gives the ideal of romantic love a quality that brings it into closer alignment with the goal of scientific research. The latter relies on the idea of eternity in both senses of the word. So, in a way, does the former. The analogy is distant. But it is not, I think, wholly frivolous. It captures a striking feature of the experience of love when it is shaped by romantic beliefs.

Romantic love sets an unattainable goal. Approximation is all that lies within our power. But coming closer means more than seeing the individuality of those we love with greater vividness and affection. It means believing, with increasing fervor, that the world as we know it would be incomplete without our love; that the nonexistence of the one is as unthinkable as that of the other; that if anything cannot not be, it is our love for one another. At the end of this endless process of deepening love, could we ever reach it, the contingency of loving the particular people we do would be converted to a destiny, as lovers call it—just as, by analogy, every correlation would be converted to a cause, could we ever fully satisfy our desire to know.

The impossibility of completing this conversion is obvious to everyone engaged in scientific research. But here, the goal is at least intelligible. In love, it is difficult even to say what converting the accidents of love to a destiny means. Yet something of this ambition is present here too—only a shadow, perhaps, of its much stronger scientific expression, but still a part of the meaning of love, when the yearning for completion remains after the hope of completion is gone.

Literary representations of the longing to see the accidents of love under the sign of necessity often draw on the image of heaven. Its Christian associations imply a state of fulfillment that romantic love rules out. Still, it is the best image we have in our cultural repertoire. If we keep its limitations in mind, it helps express the most improbable side of the unattainable ideal of romantic love.

At the end of Thomas Mann's *Buddenbrooks,* the family whose rise and fall the reader has followed through four generations lies in ruins. Death, insanity, and despair have done their work. Yet the last words of the novel express a resolute hope.

"Tom, father, grandfather, and all the others. Where have they all gone?" Frau Permaneder asks. "We shall see them no more. Oh, how hard and sad it all is." "We shall see them again," Friederike Buddenbrook replies. "Yes, that's what they say . . . if only it were so."

Then Theresa Weichbrodt, the oldest surviving member of the family, "raised herself up to the table, as high as she could. She stood on her tiptoes, craned her neck, and rapped on the tabletop—and her bonnet quivered on her head. '*It is so!*' she said with all her strength, and dared them with her eyes."[30]

The family *will* be together again, Theresa says, because it *must,* because any relationships other than these, with their unique mix of anguish and love, are absolutely unthinkable. They cannot not be.

The 1984 film *Places in the Heart* chronicles a series of affectionate, bitter, loyal, and disloyal relationships in a small Texas town during the Depression. There is murder, adultery, and uncommon kindness. In the last scene, all the characters, living and dead, criminals and victims, those who have gone some way in the path of love and those who have stumbled and fallen, are together for the one and only time in the film, taking communion in a small country church.

The scene is moving, though its meaning is obscure. Part of what it means, perhaps, is that like Theresa, the characters in the film cannot exist apart from those with whom their lives are most intimately entangled—and that heaven would be for them to have the endless time they need to comprehend the destiny that joins them.[31]

The scene is set in a church. It implies the Christian hope for redemption. But this does not deprive it of its power to express the most obscure yet not wholly unfamiliar part of love's longing, when the Christian ideal of love is brought down to earth and the timelessness of heaven becomes a goal we can neither reach nor abandon.

3

Illusions of Fulfillment

WE FEEL A KINSHIP WITH other animals. We, too, experience pleasure and pain. We grow up, grow old, and die. We reproduce and leave offspring behind. Like all living things, we are caught in the music of time.

Yet we alone know that our lives will come to an end. Knowing this, we also know that time never ends. The idea of endless time frees us to imagine goals that cannot be reached in any period of time. It arouses desires that can never be satisfied no matter how long the human adventure continues. This means that our condition is one of deep disappointment.

For some, this is an unbearable conclusion. They cannot believe that we shall never reach the highest goals that human beings can set. They refuse to accept the permanency of this self-imposed defeat.

Every life is littered with disappointments of an ordinary kind. I fail to win a promotion or attract the woman I've met on a blind date. Rain spoils my picnic; a recession depletes my IRA. We accept these disappointments as a normal part of life.

Whatever pain they bring is dulled by the thought that I can do better next time. I can look for a job where I'm more likely to succeed. I can use a different dating service. I can pay closer attention to the weather and shift my investments from stocks to bonds. The fact that things might have turned out differently and that I can often take steps to avoid future failure is a source of mental and practical relief.

Deep disappointment is different. There is no plan of attack I can invent to avoid it. Frustration is built into the nature of the goals that produce it. This is intolerable in a special way. A goal we cannot help longing to reach, yet cannot possibly attain, gives rise to a species of unhappiness that differs from the banal and partly remediable kind. One might call it "tragic" to indicate its inevitable and self-inflicted character. Unhappiness of this sort is not a challenge calling for a practical response. It is a destiny or fate.

Confronted with such a fate, it is natural that we should wish to escape it. In theory, there are two ways of doing this. One is to suppress the longing for goals beyond our grasp. But this cannot be done. The longing is too intimately connected to our most distinctively human pursuits. Science and love are inconceivable without it. So are philosophy and art. The desire to reach goals that exceed our mortal powers is woven through so many strands of experience and culture that repressing it— were such a thing even possible—would amount to the obliteration of human life as we know it.

The alternative is to persuade ourselves that the goals we seek are not in fact unattainable. This is what the evangelical Christianity my mother was taught as a child promises its followers. It tells them they shall have eternal life if they obey God's commands. My mother grasped the antihumanistic implications of this promise. She saw that it is incompatible with the acceptance of the human condition as our fate. This was the instinct that drew her to the existentialism she embraced as an adult. She felt it long before she knew what Sartre and Camus say.

The promise of a rescue from deep disappointment is not, however, a peculiar feature of the superstitious religion my grandmother tried to impose on her independent-minded daughter. It is not a sign of ignorance or laziness. The promise lies at the heart of the two highly evolved and intellectually sophisticated traditions of thought whose complex interactions, over centuries of time, have shaped the whole of Western philosophy.

One is the tradition of pagan rationalism. The other is that of biblical creationism. These differ profoundly but share the hopeful teaching that our longing for eternity can indeed be fulfilled. The belief that it can is the central message of the two most fully worked-out views of human life that Western philosophy offers those who search its treasures to find a satisfying answer to the question of how we should understand the human condition and our place in the cosmic order of things.

Those who are determined, like my mother, to hold on to our humanity, with its fateful disquietude, rather than relinquish it for the sake of a comforting illusion, have grounds to reject both views. Most of my highly educated, disbelieving friends fall in this group. They have the courage to decline the seductive invitations of both Athens and Jerusalem, and the opposed but equally consoling Gods these represent.

But are they right to conclude that their humanism requires no God at all? Here is where we part company.

To explain the experience of deep disappointment, coupled with that of joyful advance, we must, I think, assume that the world is both inherently and infinitely divine. We need this idea of God to account for the possibility of our most characteristically human experience. This God differs from those of

Athens and Jerusalem. It is less familiar and more difficult to grasp. Yet we need this other, stranger God to understand the human condition. We need it to explain who we are. First, though, we have to break the spell of the antihumanistic Gods whose illusory promises of fulfillment have kept the Western philosophical imagination in thrall from the start.

Half the people in the world who say they have any religious beliefs at all belong to one of the three Abrahamic religions. The percentage is much higher in the West and Middle East. To most of those who live in these parts of the world, the word *God* means the God of Abraham. This is the God they have in mind when they either affirm or deny his existence.

Many Christians, Jews, and Muslims identify with their religions in name only. Others are more devout. Within each tradition there are further divisions: Catholics and Protestants, Sunni and Shia, Reform Jews and Hasids. But all these groups share a broadly similar conception of God. They are the often quarrelsome members of a single family, whose disagreements are so fierce because they have so much in common, a phenomenon that in another context Freud famously described as "the narcissism of small differences."[1]

The God of Abraham is an omnipotent creator. He has the power to bring whatever he chooses into being from nothing. He is also perfectly self-sufficient. He depends on nothing before, beyond, or outside himself in order to exist. He is the "source" or "ground" or "cause" of his own being. The God of Abraham exists *because* he is God. It is part of his essence to do so.

This is true only of God. Nothing else exists by definition. Even the most lasting things in the world—the rhythms of natural life, the planets and stars, the basic laws of motion themselves—might not be, or be other than they are.

The same is true of the world as a whole. Its existence is conditional and dependent. The world exists only because God freely chose to bring it into being in the first place. The opening chapters of Genesis express this idea with poetic grandeur.

The idea of divine creation opens a chasm between God and the world—between creator and creature. It divides all reality into two opposing realms. One is defined by the absence of time and the other by its ubiquitous presence; human beings, alone among God's creatures, awkwardly straddle the two.

The first of these is the Kingdom of God. God exists by necessity. His existence is therefore unconditioned by time. There is no "before" and "after" in the Kingdom of God. This is difficult, perhaps impossible to portray. No story, which unfolds in time, or philosophical argument, which proceeds by successive steps, or painting, which uses movement and passion to convey its theme, can capture the exemption from time that defines the Kingdom of God.

The second realm is that of worldly things. It includes the whole of God's creation. Its boundaries increase as our view of the universe expands. The earth and everything on it belong to God's creation. So do the distant galaxies that our radio telescopes now allow us to see.

Everything that is created depends for its existence on something that precedes it. This is true even of human creations. The cake a baker creates would not exist but for the baker, who combines various materials according to a recipe of some kind.

God's creation is like the baker's in one way. He "comes before" the thing that he creates, just as the baker does. In another way, though, God's creativity is far greater. Unlike human artisans, who always start with materials on hand, God brings the world into being from nothing. Moreover, God himself is uncreated. He never "comes to be." God is the source of his own existence; the baker is not. The baker comes from his parents. He owes his existence to something other than himself, just as his cake does.

This is true of everything in the realm of worldly things. Every object or event in the world "comes to be" from something else. Each therefore takes time. It takes an hour to bake a cake. It takes nine months for a human embryo to grow in its mother's womb. It even takes time for a mathematician to learn a timeless truth.

The world as a whole "comes to be," too. Before God created the world, there was nothing. Then God spoke, and the world came into being. The language of Genesis invites us to think of this as an event in time, like the baking of a cake or birth of a child. This presents enormous philosophical difficulties. If the world was created in time, was there a time before it came into being? If so, what was happening then? Some theologians solve the problem by saying that God created time too—that the creation of the world and time are one and the same thing.[2] Others speculate that God might have chosen to create the world the "moment" he himself began to exist. If that were true, since God has no beginning in time, the world would have none either.[3]

Even on this view, though, the world cannot exist without God's support. It still depends on God's creative agency. And since God is free to withdraw his support whenever he chooses, the existence of the world remains vulnerable to change or extinction.

Whether the world was created at a certain moment, or has always existed, there is no guarantee that it will continue to exist for another minute, let alone last forever, as God by definition must. However one views it, the world is haunted by the specter of time. Everything in God's creation is under the sway of "coming to be and passing away." This is the defining characteristic of the realm of worldly things.

Human beings are no exception. Like all God's creatures, we are exposed to the wasting powers of time. We flit across the stage like the plants and animals around us, like the earth beneath our feet and the stars overhead in the sky.

Still, we occupy a privileged position in the theater of time. God created everything in the world but chose to make us alone in his "image."

We resemble God in a way that nothing else does. He gave us immortal souls and the knowledge that we possess them. He commands us to obey his laws and endows us with a measure of the freedom he enjoys so that we may choose to obey or disobey him freely. God promises that if we obey, he will reward us. He assures us that with his help, we shall overcome the travails of worldly existence. God subjects us to special duties and offers in return a form of deliverance for which we alone, among all his creatures, have reason to hope.

We are dual citizens who belong to two realms. One is that of the world. The world is full of disappointments. It has its pleasures as well, but none of these lasts. The supreme disappointment is death. Whatever love we find, whatever measure of joy we experience, is short-lived. This is true of other living things, too. But only we know it. The knowledge of our mortality casts a pall over everything we do and experience.

We have this knowledge because, though we belong to the world, we do not belong to it completely. We are members of the Kingdom of God, too—exiled, perhaps, and on probation, but elevated by virtue of our citizenship in this second realm to a vantage point that no other creature enjoys. In the world but not wholly of it, we can see and judge what we do

and suffer here, in the realm of time, from a vantage point unconditioned by time.

When we do, our lives are bound to appear wanting. This
is a special form of suffering that human beings alone experience. But the same perspective, from which our mortal lives
appear so small, gives us a glimmer of something infinitely
greater. Life on earth looks so deficient only because we can
form the idea of eternity, even if we cannot picture what it
looks like. The idea of eternity is one we possess because we
have already been admitted, in an incomplete and provisional
way, to the eternal Kingdom of God.

This is what it means to be made in God's image. The
relation between an original and its image is asymmetric. The
first can exist without the second but not vice versa. Still, an
image must contain something of its original or else it would
not be an image at all.

This is how it is with man's relation to God. We have
something of God in us, but not the whole of God, not God
himself. God cannot not be. Our nonbeing, by contrast, is perfectly thinkable, and what being we enjoy, so long as we remain in the realm of worldly things, is shockingly brief. Still,
we have the idea of God's eternal existence. We can grasp it
with our minds. In this imperfect but important respect, we
resemble our creator, in the way even a poor portrait resembles its subject.

Seeing how flawed we are by comparison with our creator, we cannot help yearning for something better than the
worldly state we now enjoy. We long to be more like God, to
join him in his Kingdom, beyond corruption and death—
beyond time itself, which is the source of all our suffering.

Our condition at present is one of exile or pilgrimage.
Wanting what we do, we can never be entirely at home in the
world. We are transients passing through on our way to some-

thing better. God promises those who love and obey him a homecoming of this kind. His promise inspires and guides those who are open to it, at every step along life's journey. Woe to those who think they can find what they want in the empty satisfactions the world has to offer! Woe to those who refuse God's promise and settle down in the world as if it were their home!

The result is a radical devaluation of everything the world contains. Very few human beings are able to achieve, let alone sustain, an attitude of this kind. Yet the theology of creation, to which half the world subscribes, sets it up as an ideal. It divides reality into two distinct realms, one temporal and the other eternal, and instructs its followers to work with all their might to secure God's promise to join him in the second. The division is particularly pronounced in Christianity and Islam. Even in Judaism, it grows sharper after the destruction of the Second Temple, which compelled the Jews to postpone indefinitely their worldly aspirations in favor of messianic hopes of an otherworldly kind.[4]

The Abrahamic religions paint a familiar picture of human experience. We are caught in time yet can conceive of what is not. The knowledge of death, which sets us apart from other animals, already contains the idea of eternity and arouses the longing to reach it.

But Judaism, Christianity, and Islam do more than accept this general portrait of the human condition. They place it within an explanatory frame whose effect is to eliminate the possibility of deep disappointment.

To the question, "Why are we exposed to the danger of such disappointment?" the Abrahamic religions answer, "On account of our own actions." They make the danger *our* responsibility. They *moralize* it.

The gap between our mortal state and our immortal dreams is not, they say, a fate we simply suffer. It is the price we pay for our misdeeds. In the harshest Christian version, these are crimes. In the gentler version of Islam, they are acts of forgetfulness; in Judaism, of promise breaking. In each case, our unhappiness in being cut off from the eternity of the Kingdom of God is the result of something we have done, or failed to do, or are doing now. It is our *fault*.

In one way, this makes our condition worse. It is bad enough to be in it. That we are the cause of our own suffering adds to its awfulness. But in another way, it offers a ray of hope. If we are responsible for getting ourselves into this predicament, perhaps we can do something to get ourselves out of it. Perhaps human agency has a role to play in overcoming our deep disappointment, even if we cannot do this entirely on our own.

Our moral powers give us, in fact, more than a bare hope of escaping the special unhappiness that deep disappointment entails. We have the secure expectation that we *shall* escape it, so long as we exercise our freedom in the right way. The security of this expectation is founded on God's benevolence.

God is all-powerful. There is nothing he cannot do. But God is also all-good. He is incapable of wickedness or deceit. We can therefore be sure that God will use his boundless power for beneficent ends.

This applies with particular force to God's human creatures. God's interest in us is uniquely strong. We thus have reason to be confident that whatever our past failings, a renewed commitment to obey God and to love him with all our hearts will be met with divine solicitude. (Augustine's predestinarian theology, which Luther enthusiastically embraced, breaks this chain of reasoning by exalting God's power at the expense of his benevolence, with important consequences for the fate of religious belief in the mostly Christian West.)[5]

God's affection for us gives him the motive to lift the threat of deep disappointment. His infinite power gives him the ability to do so. It is unimaginable that God would want his most beloved creatures to suffer this peculiarly agonizing fate, or be powerless to relieve them of it. Those who act as God directs can therefore be assured that one day, somehow, they will possess the eternal prize that lies beyond their reach on this side of the grave. They may not be able to conceive how this will happen or what the experience will be like. But they know with certainty that if they follow the path God lights, they shall have what they can never find in the realm of time.

The faithful are able to work toward this goal in a deliberate way, just as they make plans to avoid disappointments of an ordinary kind. This is the promise the Abrahamic religions make to their followers. It is the source of their lasting appeal.

But understanding the appeal is one thing and yielding to it is another. For those who view deep disappointment as an ineradicable feature of the human condition, the divinely sanctioned promise that we shall overcome it amounts to the belief that one day this most human form of suffering will no long plague us because . . . we shall no longer be human at all. The Abrahamic religions invite us to make the trade. Millions of believers think it a bargain. My mother declined to accept it and so do most of my friends. They would rather stay with their humanity than dream it away. So would I.

The dream may bring a kind of peace. But those who dream it continue to be human, even as they do. They cannot escape the special kind of disappointment that comes with their condition merely by imagining themselves no longer in it. They cannot extinguish the knowledge they are dreaming.

A dreamer knows that he or she is dreaming only if the dreamer is already awake. For my part, I would never sacrifice the light of wakefulness, however brief, for the solace of a dream, however great. That is a narcotic temptation. I prefer living with disappointment to the comfort of a God who promises relief, but only on the condition that I relinquish my humanity—not today perhaps, but in that final state of consummated bliss that represents the sum of all my longings.

The temptation to accept the bargain on these terms is itself part of our humanity. We feel it only because we long for what we can approach but never reach in time. But yielding to the temptation is not a way of understanding the meaning of this longing. Nor is it an answer to the question of what we must assume about the world as a whole in order to explain how this most human of all our longings is possible at all. It is an evasion of the question instead.

The doctrine of creation is inherently irrational. This is not because God's reasons for creating the world are more complex than our minds can comprehend. The problem lies deeper. If God's will is truly free, then his creation of the world *must* be unintelligible.

Suppose God had reasons for creating the world when and as he did, though our minds are too limited to understand them. In that case, God's act of creation is intelligible, in principle at least. But it is also constrained. It is led and shaped by the reasons that guide it. How can God's will be free if it is confined in this way?

One response is that even if God's creation of the world was guided by reasons, he was free to follow these reasons or not. God might have chosen to follow other reasons or none. He might have chosen not to create a world at all.

But, then, did God have reasons for preferring one set of reasons to another? For choosing a rational course rather than an irrational one? Did God have reasons for deciding to create a world in the first place, instead of leaving things as they were, in a formless void?

If he did, then God's decision is once again intelligible, but, again, beholden to reason. Dependence is the price that must be paid for intelligibility. The pattern repeats itself no matter how far back we pursue our inquiry into the mystery of creation.

The upshot is that for God's will to be perfectly free, it cannot be under any direction at all, including that of reason. It cannot be preceded by anything other than itself, even by reasons that guide and explain it. God's will must be perfectly spontaneous. But this means that it must also be completely unintelligible. We can never *think* our way to an understanding of the idea of divine creation. We have to accept it on *faith*.

This is part of the meaning of the saying that there is a quarrel between Athens and Jerusalem.

The philosopher seeks to understand the world by the light of reason alone. He refuses to make the sacrifice of intellect that faith demands. From the standpoint of the Abrahamic religions, the philosopher's refusal reflects a shocking overconfidence in his unassisted human powers. Augustine condemned the philosophers of Greece and Rome for their belief in the sufficiency of reason. They were, he said, the victims of their own deluded pride.[6]

Christianity, Judaism, and Islam have had their great philosophers—Augustine, Aquinas, Maimonides, Crescas, Avicenna, and Al-Ghazali, among many. Yet all worked within the framework of faith. Some attributed greater power to reason than others. But all felt constrained by the limits the doctrine of creation places on rational explanation in general. The challenge was to go as far as reason allows while accepting God's

creation of the world as a truth that reason can neither establish nor refute.

Philosophers working outside this framework have felt
no such constraint. This is most obviously true of those who
lived before the Abrahamic religions captured the imagination
of philosophers and ordinary people alike, and came to dom-
inate the terms on which the questions of philosophy were
henceforth pursued in those portions of the earth where these
religions held sway.

The philosophers of Greece and Rome were unconcerned
to square their teachings with a doctrine of creation that in its
Abrahamic form lay beyond the horizon of their thought and
experience. Yet as the philosophies of Plato and Aristotle show,
the spirit of Athens, as much as that of Jerusalem, leads to a
view of the world that explains away the human experience of
deep disappointment.

Plato and Aristotle offer accounts of the world that leave
no place for this experience as a fateful feature of the human
condition. Moved by the need to rid us of a phenomenon
whose very existence they viewed as an affront to reason, the
greatest philosophers of pagan antiquity constructed a picture
of reality in which deep disappointment does not, indeed cannot, exist in a final and absolute sense. Despite their boundless
commitment to reason, or rather precisely because of it, the
thinkers who gave a start to the entire tradition of Western
philosophy arrived at the same conclusion as their Abrahamic successors, who, while confining reason in the name of
faith, wrote deep disappointment out of the human condition
as well.

The Abrahamic religions have a mass following. Philosophy has always been an esoteric pursuit. But the narrow path
of philosophy is equally capable of leading the few who follow

it to the same consoling thought that deep disappointment is not our ineluctable fate.

Not every philosopher has arrived at this conclusion, nor does the very nature of philosophy dictate that one must. But the temptation is always there, and always very strong. Just how strong is suggested by the teachings of the two Greek thinkers between whose views so much of Western philosophy has oscillated ever since.

One of the most remarkable passages in all of Plato's writings occurs midway through the *Republic*.[7]

Socrates and a group of young men have been discussing the nature of justice as a trait of character and a property of political regimes. This has led them to a philosophical question about the nature of reality. What is really real and what only seemingly so? Socrates illustrates his answer in a series of brilliant metaphors. The most famous is the so-called parable of the cave.

Picture men seated on a bench deep in a cave, Socrates begins. Imagine them chained in place, looking at shadows cast on the wall before them by puppets carried on sticks behind their backs, in front of a fire the men cannot see because their heads are fastened forward. "What a strange image," one of Socrates' companions remarks. "Yes," Socrates replies. "It looks remarkably like us."

The prisoners in Socrates' cave are recognizably human. They are more than animals. They hold contests to see who best remembers the sequence of the images appearing before them. Those who do are given prizes.

The winners have outstanding memories. They excel at distinguishing "before" and "after" and identifying the relations between them. This is the beginning of a kind of science. It is the origin of all causal reasoning, which seeks to explain

what happens in time by identifying a regular order in the succession of events.

Any attempt to do this, no matter how primitive, already
presupposes a self-conscious awareness of time. All animals
are sensitive to events and capable of developing habits in response to them, to one degree or another. But only human beings could ever stage an explanatory contest of the sort that
occupies the prisoners in Socrates' cave.

Still, the prisoners can hardly be called fulfilled human
beings. Their condition is one of ignorance and constraint.
They are laboring under an illusion. They think the shadows
on the wall before them are real. But Socrates' listeners—and
we readers—know this is a laughable mistake.

The prisoners are like dreamers who mistake their dreams
for waking life. My dog, Maisie, is dreaming her life away, too.
She lives without knowing that the world she experiences has
a reality independent of her experience of it. In this respect,
Maisie is living in a kind of cave as well. There is a difference,
though. For Maisie, there is no release from the cave in which
she dwells. Socrates' cave dwellers have the power to break the
spell, shake off the dream, and rise to waking life. This power
is already manifest in the prisoners' banter about the order of
the images on the wall, which depends on their ability to identify, recall, and describe the relation between "before" and "after."
The possibility of their liberation is there from the start. It lies
in the prisoners' distinctively human awareness of time.

The prisoners do not liberate themselves, however. Help
comes from the outside. Someone sets one of the prisoners
free from his chains. We do not know who this might be until
we get to the end of the story.

Once the prisoner is freed and can turn his head around
to see the puppets behind him, he is able to recognize that the
shadows on the wall of the cave are only the reflections or im-

ages of objects more real than themselves. To be able to draw this conclusion, he must already possess the power to see an image *as* an image.[8] This power is a kind of detachment. It is the ability to extract oneself from the enchantment of experience, with its ceaseless flow of images, and to see these from a distance: from a point of view that is no longer captive to the illusory belief that the images one is experiencing constitute the whole of reality. It is the power of *abstraction.*

When this power is exercised, a new order of reality comes into view. The prisoner who has been freed from his chains now sees that the existence of the images on the wall derives from and depends on that of the puppets at the back of the cave. He *abstracts* from these images to their source or cause. Seeing them in this new light, he is able to explain the images in a way he could not before.

Even when he was chained in place, he and the other prisoners engaged in a primitive form of abstraction by attempting to identify and name the order in which the images before them appeared. This order is something distinct from the images themselves. It possesses a different kind of reality. The prisoners are able to discern it because they already possess the knowledge that time is passing as they watch it. The liberated prisoner merely exercises this power of abstraction at a higher level. When he does, he discovers another order of reality that is superior to any the other prisoners yet suspect.

Its superiority is implied by the distinction between an image and its original. This relation is one of causal and explanatory dependence. Without the original, there would be no image, though the reverse is not the case. We can say what an image *is* only by reference to the original from which it derives. The reverse proposition is false. The relation of dependence is even deeper than this, however. It has its origin in the distinction between unity and multiplicity—between what Socrates calls the "one" and the "many." At its very deepest level, it rests on the distinction between eternity and time.

Relative to the shadows they cast on the wall of the cave, the puppets behind the prisoners "stand still." The shadow any particular puppet casts first appears, then disappears, then reappears again later on. The puppet remains the same. Its shadows are many; the puppet is one. It is the durable, unifying source of all the shadows it casts at different times. The prisoner who has been freed now understands this. He sees that the coming and going of the images before him have their cause and explanation in one unchanging thing.

This discovery has the potential to repeat itself at a higher level.

In a very basic sense, our familiar waking lives are like the dream lives of the prisoners that Socrates describes. Our world, like theirs, is a kind of theater in which one spectacle is constantly displaced by another. We are all absorbed in the show. We follow the movements of the people and things around us with rapt attention, believing they are the most real things that exist—just as the prisoners think there is no greater reality than the shadows they watch on the wall of their cave.

But this is a terrible mistake. Indeed, it is the same mistake.

The changing things we see around us in "the real world" are no more intelligible in themselves than the shadows in the cave. We can understand and explain the existence of the ordinary things that fill the world of waking life—the artifacts, institutions, and other people that surround us—only by referring their reality to something more real still, of which they are the mere images or reflections. We can say *what* these ordinary things are, and *how* they come to be, only by relating them to a higher order of reality whose fundamental characteristic is that of relative changelessness and unity vis-à-vis the

constantly moving and multiple objects of common attention—
just as the mindless experience of the prisoners becomes intelligible to them only when they discover the single, stable source
of the many flowing images that hold them in thrall.

That our condition is the same as that of the prisoners
at first seems preposterous. But this is exactly what Socrates
wants us to see. The point of his parable is that all the seemingly real things about us are only images or reflections, too;
that human wisdom begins with the search for their unmov-
ing source; and that to become wise, we must turn around, like
the prisoner freed from his chains, and look in the opposite
direction, away from the world to which we are accustomed,
toward a more lasting reality that alone can account for everything we thoughtlessly take to be real.

Once a person has experienced such a "turning about of
the soul," his appetite for knowledge can never be appeased
until he arrives at a point beyond which no further understanding is conceivable. That happens only when his mind finally grasps the one eternal source of everything that belongs
to the world of time. Nothing could be further removed from
the transience and volatility of the prisoners' experience. Yet
the capacity to reach the knowledge of eternity in which our
longing for wisdom concludes is present from the very beginning in the prisoners' peculiarly human awareness of time. It is
already at work in their rudimentary abstractions. The power
only needs to be set free. This is the extremely serious message
of Socrates' amusing tale.

Socrates briefly sketches the path a liberated soul follows
in its search for perfect knowledge. The search begins with the
insight that ordinary things (the puppets in his story) not only
cast shadows of their own but are mere shadows themselves,
that they stand in the same relation of image to original as the
shadows on the wall of the cave do to them. This leads to the

discovery of the changeless principles that give ordinary things their intelligibility and explain what it means for them to be the things they are. Socrates calls these principles the "Forms" of things.

But this discovery is only the beginning of a more arduous search. What explains the Forms of things? How can we account for *their* intelligibility? What is the source or cause of *their* existence—of their being what and as they are?

The inquiry leads up, out of the cave, into ever higher regions of thought. It comes to an end, at last, in an encounter with what Socrates calls "the Form of the Good."

Here, words nearly fail him. It is impossible to convey in anything but inadequate images (!) what the Form of the Good really is. All that Socrates can say is that it is the necessary condition for everything else. The Form of the Good, Socrates tells his astonished listeners, explains all the other Forms and everything that depends on them in turn. It is what makes the Forms intelligible. It is what causes them to exist. Beyond it, nothing more can be conceived. At this point, the soul that has turned away from the world, to follow the path of philosophy, comes to rest. Its search is at an end.

The search begins when one of the prisoners in the cave is freed from his chains and able to see the puppets behind his back. It continues with the insight that the puppets themselves are images, on up through the world of Forms to its culmination in the Form of the Good. At each stage, wisdom comes with the discovery of an unchanging reality that gives order and intelligibility to a lower level of heterogeneous and mutable things—the apprehension of a timeless "one" that directs and shapes a changing "many."

The Form of the Good is this principle of intelligibility itself. It is the very idea of timelessness and unity that makes all explanation, at every level, explicable. Nothing outside the circle of light cast by the Form of the Good has any intelligibility at all, and nothing beyond the Form of the Good is needed to explain it. It is all-illuminating and self-sufficient—unified, changeless, and perfect. It is the source of the order *in* time because it is itself *beyond* time. It is eternal and *therefore*—the fundamental Socratic equation—perfectly, indeed uniquely, real.

Even for the prisoners chained to their bench at the bottom of the cave, human life has already begun. They are sufficiently detached from the flow of images on the wall before them to be able to detect an order in their sequence. Time does not simply pass for them. They watch it passing from a distance. The prisoners have already been released from the bondage to time that holds other animals in chains from which they can never break free.

The prisoners delight in the use of their distinctively human freedom. They compete to see who among them has the strongest memory and greatest predictive powers. The winner knows more than the others do. Still, his is a pathetic kind of knowledge. It rests on an illusion—on something "unreal." But the detachment that makes it possible allows for higher forms of understanding, and the desire to know that is at work even at this primitive level inspires the search for an ever better grasp of reality, free of all illusions.

Time is change, motion, coming to be, and passing away. Reality is the timeless order in time. The progress of understanding that leads from the prisoners on their bench to the final vision of the Form of the Good lies in the ever more refined grasp of this timeless order. It is progress toward an understanding of the eternal and divine. This is the arc of the human adventure. The detachment from time that the meanest human being already enjoys is at once the condition for it and the motive to pursue the adventure to its end.

Socrates' parable concludes in a curious way.

Those who have managed through years of patient study to gain an understanding of the Form of the Good long to remain there, in the light, contemplating the final object of their search. Left to themselves, this is what they would do. But if there is to be any hope of greater enlightenment for those who remain below, the few who have escaped from the cave, and ascended to the summit of knowledge, must be compelled to go back down and share what they have discovered with the others. The parable ends by describing the frustrations of anyone who tries to do this.

Blinded by the light, he stumbles and trips over his words. He sounds like a fool to those who are more accustomed to the darkness of the cave. They mock him as an unwanted interloper. Having failed to teach them the truth, he is eventually discharged—if the prisoners do not kill him in anger—and allowed to return to the neighborhood of the Form of the Good, where he spends the rest of his days in contemplation of it.

This coda to the story of liberation underscores two lessons. The first is that only a few ever achieve it. Most people remain slaves to unreality—prisoners of illusion. They never exercise the potential for liberation that all human beings possess. The rare individual who does looks strange from their perspective. "Exiled on earth amidst its hooting crowds, he cannot walk, borne down by giant wings."[9]

The second lesson is that for the few who yearn to know, and will not give up until they do, their yearning has an attainable end.

The Form of the Good alone is perfectly real and therefore fully knowable—not in part, or only up to a point, but through and through, without deficit or remainder. By contrast, all that is multiple and changing lacks the very thing that makes anything real at all. There is therefore no need to worry about understanding the countless mutable things we see about us in the world of sights and sounds. That would be an endless task. But we are spared it because there is nothing to know about them. There is no intelligibility in them. Once we have wrapped our minds around the Form of the Good, we know all we have to know to fulfill our longing to understand.

The inspiring message of the *Republic* is that we can do this if we try.

Most of us worry about the ordinary disappointments of life. We worry about losing our money, reputation, and power. But these are ridiculous things to fret over. Only a person who is a slave to illusion would devote himself or herself to trying to avoid them.

The one disappointment that should truly concern us is the possibility of failing to satisfy our yearning to know. That would be a genuine and terrible loss. It would amount to a loss of reality itself—to dreaming one's life away in a realm of shadows.

But this disappointment—the only one that really matters —is within our power to avoid. All we have to do is keep to the path of philosophy. If we do, we can be sure that we will not be disappointed. Trivial disappointments may be unavoidable, but deep disappointment is not. With effort, we can save ourselves from it. *Save* is the verb that Socrates uses in the concluding lines of the *Republic* to emphasize that the complete satisfaction of our deepest longing lies within our reach. All we must do is grasp it.

There is a parallel here to the teaching of the Abrahamic religions, which also promise relief from the prospect of deep disappointment.

The differences, of course, are striking. For Socrates, the path to salvation is intellectual. It requires only that one think. For followers of the Abrahamic religions, salvation is a matter of obedience and will. It rests on faith. It demands a voluntary subordination to God's commands—the opposite of the prideful independence of thought.

The Socratic path is for a few. Only a small number have the intellectual stamina to pursue it. The Abrahamic religions are for the many. Their principal function is to offer relief to the masses. There is no popular version of Socrates' strenuous ascent to the Form of the Good.

Furthermore, the goal that Socrates envisions is one that can be reached, intermittently at least, even in this life, though a philosopher must await the next one to experience its uninterrupted fulfillment. For followers of the Abrahamic religions, the idea that we can hope for the complete, even if only temporary, satisfaction of our longing to be with God, so long as we inhabit our mortal bodies, is anathema. The doctrine of creation drives a wedge between the world of time and the eternal Kingdom of God. In Socrates' view, the separation between these two realms is less absolute. The Form of the Good can be seen in the illusory phantoms around us, if we only have eyes to look. It is possible to experience heaven on earth, from time to time at least. Socrates himself seems to have done so (in Plato's telling, at least).[10]

Still, despite these differences, a fundamental similarity remains. There is no more room in Socrates' philosophy for the phenomenon of deep disappointment than there is in the Abrahamic religions. Socratism and Abrahamism eliminate its possibility in different, even antithetical ways. But the result is the same. In each case, we are told—promised—that we can escape this particularly awful form of suffering through an effort of our own, moral or intellectual. We are taught how to save ourselves from the human condition.

This condition may be described as that of "fallen Man" or of "the prisoners in a cave." There is something terrible about it. It seems to show a gap between what we most want and what, even with our greatest efforts, we are able to achieve. But the gap is not permanent. It is not inscribed in the nature of things. It is possible to overcome it. This is the good news the religions of Abraham deliver to millions of believers, who count on God's help to save them, and Plato's philosophy, to a proud and self-sufficient few. That such radically different paths lead to the same end suggests the strength of the longing to reach it.

Plato was a student of Socrates and Aristotle of Plato. They form the triumvirate that heads the parade of Western philosophy.

Aristotle's view of the world is in many respects fundamentally different from that of his teacher. He came to it through a critical reflection on the principles of Platonism. Yet Aristotle, too, arrives at the conclusion that deep disappointment is inconceivable. Indeed, one might say that the whole of Aristotle's un-Platonic philosophy is constructed to guarantee this Platonic result.

Different philosophers are struck by different things. Their imaginations lead them in different directions. Plato was captivated by mathematics. He was impressed by the special sort of necessity that mathematical reasoning involves. Aristotle took his point of departure from the world of living things. He was curious about plants and animals and studied them closely. He wanted to know why they move in the ways they do. This question was of more than limited interest to Aristotle. It shaped his entire way of thinking and conditioned the answers he gave to the most fundamental questions of philosophy.[11]

Nowhere are the consequences of Aristotle's biological imagination clearer than in a casual remark he makes in his treatise *On the Soul*.

All living beings, Aristotle says, do two things. They take in nourishment (we would say "metabolize") and reproduce. Some animals do much more than this, but all plants and animals, even the simplest ones, engage in these two activities.

What explains them? There are many different answers. The most important one accounts for these activities in terms of their purpose or goal. It explains what they are *for*.

With respect to reproduction, Aristotle thinks the goal is clear. "The most natural thing for a living thing to do is to make another like itself, for an animal to make an animal, a plant to make a plant, in order to have a share in the everlasting and divine, so far as its nature permits."[12] This simple observation is the touchstone of Aristotle's philosophy.

Animals and plants are constantly changing—growing, dying, moving from one place to another, making copies of themselves. But change and motion are not limited to living beings. Inanimate things, like drops of water and clods of earth, disintegrate, coagulate, and change place, too. The stars and planets are the most changeless things we see. But even they move about in their orbits. Everything in the cosmos is moving in some way.

What causes these motions? What explains them? Again, there are many answers, but, again, the most important one in every case is the same as it is for plants and animals. "The most natural thing" for *any* thing to do is move in such a way that it has a share in "the everlasting and divine."

This can be put in even grander terms. In book IV of the *Physics*, Aristotle reflects at length on the nature of time.[13] What is time? His answer is that time is the "measure" of motion. Apart from motion, there is no such thing as time. Motions are defined by the time they take to complete. Time and motion are conceptually joined. If everything that moves does so for the sake of participating in what is "everlasting" and therefore timeless, then the purpose or goal of all that happens *in* time is to possess a "share" of what is *not*.

Some things have a greater share than others. But nothing is excluded altogether or—so long as it remains in motion—able to leave time completely behind. This is the universal fate of all natural beings: to yearn for a timelessness they can never possess without qualification, but subject always to the limitations that define what things of their kind are able to do.

It is a mistake, though, to think of these limitations as a source of disappointment. It is not a disappointment, in Aristotle's view, to be able to do only what one's nature equips one to do. This is just the way things are. And if nothing in the world is set up to reach eternity in an absolutely unqualified sense, everything is capable of fully achieving the share its nature permits. "Nature does nothing in vain."[14]

It is also a mistake to imagine the eternity that every moving thing is striving to reach as a world beyond this one—a "heaven" beyond the "earth." For Aristotle, there is only one world, this world, the all-comprehending cosmos that stretches from the highest to the lowest things we see. Beyond it there is nothing, not even empty space. The very idea of anything beyond the world is incoherent. It makes neither logical nor physical sense. The eternity that things in the world all long to reach is internal to the world itself. It is the built-in goal of worldly striving. Aristotle's eternal God is the indwelling principle of time, not a creator outside it.

This is a challenging idea. Aristotle does his best to explain it in his treatise on *Metaphysics,* where in chapter 12 he offers an account of what he calls the "unmoved mover."[15]

Later readers, influenced by the doctrine of creation, have been tempted to interpret Aristotle's unmoved mover as an anticipation of the supernatural God of Abraham, just as they have been tempted to construe Plato's Form of the Good in a similar way. In Plato's case, there is perhaps more justification for this. In Aristotle's there is none. The unmoved mover is the name he gives to the divinity of the world itself, whose eternal order is self-sufficient and self-contained.

In this respect, Aristotle is the pagan philosopher par excellence. Some of the greatest thinkers in the Christian, Muslim, and Jewish traditions embraced many of his ideas. But they could never accept the fundamental premise on which his view of the world is based without abandoning their belief in the God of Genesis, who exists before the world and beyond it, and freely wills it into being from nothing.

Aristotle's account of the human condition fits seamlessly into his pagan cosmology.

Everything in the world has a distinctive nature of some kind. Human beings are no exception. Like other animals, we eat and grow and mate and die. But there are two things that we alone do. One is live in cities. The other is pursue a reflective understanding of the world as a whole—as distinct from merely adjusting to the demands of our local environment in a habitual way.

These two activities require the use of a power that, among all the plants and animals on earth, only we possess. Aristotle calls it the power of "reason."[16] City building and scientific inquiry display our rationality in particularly vivid ways, though the power they reveal suffuses every corner of human experience, to one degree or another.

Aristotle imagines the power of reason in the same way that Socrates does in the parable of the cave. He thinks of it as a power of detachment—the ability to "abstract" oneself from the flow of time and see the course of events from a perspective outside it.

City building is a case in point. Some other animals—bees and termites, for example—live in communities, too. These also have a governing order. But the order of a human city (what we call its "constitution") is constructed with deliberate foresight by the people who inhabit it. They do not just *have* a constitution. They consciously *construct* it according to a plan.

Karl Marx captures this distinction in a famous aphorism. "The worst of architects," he says, "differs from the best of bees in this—that he erects in his mind, before he begins, an idea of the building he means to construct."[17] This requires the ability to "look ahead," to imagine what does not yet exist. That is possible only because the architect who plans his building possesses the universal human power of abstraction that liberates him, like the prisoners in Socrates' cave, from the bondage to time that is the permanent fate of other living things.

Possessing this power, we want to exercise it. In this respect, we are no different from other animals. A squirrel has certain distinctive powers, too—most important, the power to make another squirrel. It yearns to exercise these powers, to be all that a squirrel can be. It is in its nature to seek the kind of fulfillment its nature allows. The same is true of human beings. We are able to live in cities because we possess the foresight that enables us to fashion rules by which to critically judge our own conduct. Having this power, we want to put it into play. We want to *activate* it. Being unable to do so would frustrate a natural drive. This is the meaning of Aristotle's famous remark that to live outside a city, one must be either a "beast" or a "god."[18]

We have no reason to doubt that this drive can be fulfilled. So far as the work of politics is concerned, there is nothing that prevents us from reaching our goal. It is true that no city lasts forever. Every political community is subject to the same forces of dissolution that rule our individual lives. But to wish to build an immortal city is foolish. It asks more than our nature allows. It ignores the limits within which human reason is confined by our hybrid nature as rational *animals*.

It is also true that the enterprise of city building can go off the rails for all sorts of accidental reasons. There are countless ways in which the attempt to establish or maintain a constitution may fail. Aristotle describes a number of familiar sources of disintegration.[19] But these are ordinary disappointments, not deep ones. They do not point to any inherent incapacity in our power to do what we find fulfillment in doing. In the realm of political action, the way is open to our being all that human nature equips and bids us to be.

The same is true of scientific inquiry.

Science is the search for explanations—for an account of why things happen as they do. Explanation begins with observation. We must perceive things before we can explain them. Other animals possess the power of perception. They are predisposed to react in certain ways to what they see and feel. A few animals are able to develop more elaborate habits based on these predispositions. Domesticated animals, for example, can be trained to follow very elaborate routines. But only we advance from perception to explanation—from observation to science. That is because we alone possess the power of abstraction that enables us to take this remarkable step.

We explain a particular event by bringing it under a general rule of some kind. I see a squirrel climb a tree. I explain its movements on various grounds. I say that squirrels climb trees because predators chase them up, because their limbs equip them to climb, and because they want to eat the nuts at the top. The movements of this particular squirrel, which I see with my eyes, are explicable because they exemplify a set of rules that I grasp through a process of mental abstraction from what I perceive.

The generalizations that explain the behavior of the squirrel I see climbing a tree are all gathered, for Aristotle, under a single master principle. Squirrels do the things they characteristically do on account of their *nature.*

Each species possesses a nature of its own—squirrels one kind, blackbirds another, oak trees a third, and so on. The nature of any particular kind of thing is manifest in the actions of every member of that kind, no two of which are exactly alike. Their nature is what these individual actions have in common; it is what informs and guides them.

We are able to explain what we perceive because we have the power to "look through" the countless manifestations of any particular nature and with our mind's eye see the general rule or principle that unites them. The ability to do this is the one that Socrates depicts, with a literary flourish, as the power to see an image as an image. Aristotle goes to great lengths to explain how this power works—how we get from the perception of individual beings to an understanding of their general nature—but he is compelled to assume, as Socrates must, that the ability to cross this divide is already there, as a liberating potential, in the eyes with which we look on the world in the first place, insofar as these are human eyes at all.[20]

We possess this power by nature, just as squirrels possess the power to climb trees. Possessing it, we want to use it. We are naturally inclined to want to explain the things we see. We compulsively inquire into the natural order of things so as to be able to account for the variety of motions, actions, and events we observe in the cosmos around us. Nothing falls outside the range of our speculative hunger.

At the first level of inquiry—roughly, the investigations that Aristotle identifies with the natural sciences—this hunger can be fulfilled. Our minds equip us to grasp the natures of all the things we see, if we pay careful attention. We are set up for success.

When this work is done, we understand all that can be understood about the things we have studied with care. There is always more to perception than to cognition. But the excess is not intelligible. It is a brute fact that cannot be explained. Once we have grasped the natures of things, we can be confident that there is nothing more to know about them. Our longing to know is—almost—at an end.

One last question, though, remains to be answered before this longing is completely fulfilled. If the natures of things, which we grasp by a process of abstraction, explain everything that can be explained in our perceptions of them, what explains these natures themselves? How can we account for the fact that the world in which we find ourselves is explicable at all?

It is characteristic that Aristotle does not dismiss this question as an idle or unanswerable one. He thinks it supremely important and believes it has a definitive answer.

His answer is as follows. Everything in the world moves for the sake of acquiring a share in the everlasting and divine. The nature of a thing is its particular "style" of sharing. All its movements are intelligible because they are directed toward this goal. The ultimate object of these movements, though, is not itself set or drawn in motion by something else. Its existence is wholly self-contained. It is the source of its own being. It is not a creator who exists apart from the world. But like the more familiar God to whom Jews, Christians, and Muslims pray, Aristotle's unmoved mover is defined by the fact that it cannot not exist. If this were not the case—if the unmoved mover owed its existence to something else—the explanation of any movement in the world could never come to an end and therefore, in Aristotle's view, never establish anything conclusive at all.

If we grant that the world is to any degree intelligible—and who but a madman can doubt it?—then Aristotle thinks we are bound to assume that the natures of things are themselves ultimately explained by reference to a force or power that is self-explanatory because it exists of necessity. Aristotle's unmoved mover, for whose sake everything else moves as it does, ensures that the world is accessible to our understanding not just *provisionally* or *contingently*. It guarantees that the world *must* be intelligible *if* we are to be able to understand *anything* about it at all (as we obviously do).

With this, our quest for knowledge is at an end. There are no further questions to ask. The human longing to know is now as fully satisfied as it could possibly be, not just for us, but for any rational being with the power to grasp the natures of things in the emancipating light of reason.

To be sure, our desire to know may be thwarted in countless ways. We may be disabled or poor or distracted by physical pleasure or never find the teacher we need. But there is nothing in the nature of the desire, or its object, or the relation between them that guarantees failure. For Aristotle, this is a truth of universal application. The desires that define the natures of different kinds of things are often frustrated by accidental causes but never by nature itself. A squirrel may be struck by lightning and fall to the ground but cannot fail to reach its goal because it is a squirrel and not a gopher. The same is true of the human desire to know. Shallow disappointments abound for us as well, but deep disappointment does not exist. What we long to have we shall possess, with perseverance and a bit of luck.

Of course we can enjoy the knowledge we yearn to possess only within the limits of the human condition, just as we can only build cities that remain hostage to our animal needs (what today we call "economic" necessity).

Aristotle compares the experience of a man who, after years of study, at last knows all there is to know about the world to that of a god. The man's knowledge makes him divine. He becomes as eternal as the object of his thinking, so long as he continues to think about it.[21]

He cannot do this forever, though. To begin with, he is mortal. His life, and therefore his thinking, must one day come to an end. Moreover, even while he lives, his thinking cannot be sustained at full tilt all the time. The greatest human thinker has bodily needs that must be met. These require that he interrupt his thinking, from time to time, for nourishment and rest. He also needs the company of others. He enjoys their humor, warmth, and support. He is a member of a political community with responsibilities that draw him away from his philosophical pursuits. A human being who longs to understand the world has the power to do so completely, but can sustain this state of perfect knowledge only with interruptions and for a while.

In this respect, his situation is only "like" that of a god. The gods are able to engage continuously and forever in an activity we experience episodically at best. That is because, though we have the divine power of thought, we also have bodies that die.

This is not the best condition we can imagine. There are better things in the world than us.[22] But it is *our* condition. Should we be disappointed that we are not gods but only godlike? That would be an unnatural wish. We have the nature we do. It equips us to share in the everlasting and divine in a particular way—the human way. Our longing to do this can be gratified entirely, subject only to the limitations that constrain us as metabolic and political beings. This is the order of the world. There is no deep disappointment anywhere we look. That things do not always go as we wish is obvious. But there are no built-in roadblocks in the way of our becoming all our nature allows us to be.

The knowledge that this is so produces a kind of contentment. Aristotle's panoramic picture of the world is constructed to ensure that we are at peace with our fate. Nothing could be further from the view that deep disappointment is the essence of our uneasy condition.

The thought that we are bound to be disappointed in the pursuit of our highest ambitions is more than a little disturbing. To many, it seems absurd. How could this even be possible? It *must* be otherwise. The world *has* to be arranged in such a way that the gap between longing and achievement can be closed.

This "must" is pre-philosophical. It is a psychological imperative. The pictures of the world that guarantee that deep disappointment does not exist are its highly refined expressions.

There are many pictures of this kind. Buddhism offers one, with its promise of release from the wheel of reincarnation and the endless cycle of suffering.[23] In the West, two visions of the world have played a lasting role in assuring us that deep disappointment is not our permanent fate. They are associated with the names of two cities, Athens and Jerusalem.

The latter signifies the family of Abrahamic religions, with their creationist theologies and promise of a life to come in which our yearning to be with God will at last be fulfilled, on the condition that we behave ourselves and follow God's commands. The idea of an all-powerful and beneficent God makes this result more than plausible. It guarantees it.

Athens signifies the rationalism of pagan philosophy, as exemplified in the works of Plato and Aristotle. Unlike the Abrahamic religions, which demand a sacrifice of the intellect, the philosophies of Plato and Aristotle rest on the assumption that our minds are equipped to answer every question we are capable of asking. They start from an exuberant embrace of the power of thought, as opposed to its restriction in the name of faith. Others have followed their lead. Plotinus, Spinoza, and Hegel are (complicated) examples.

This is not a path for everyone. As Spinoza says at the end of the *Ethics,* only a few ever find their way to it.[24] Yet for those souls that have the wings, in Plotinus's words, to fly home to "the One,"[25] the result is a state of contentment from which the prospect of deep disappointment has been banished, as surely as it has from the heaven of Abraham's children.

Millions satisfy their wish to overcome the gap between time and eternity by imagining their father in heaven. A few satisfy it by thinking their way to divine wisdom. These strategies are antithetical. But the end they seek is the same. They will never go out of fashion.

Reflecting on the meaning of Athens and Jerusalem, we face a basic choice. We can accept the experience of deep disappointment as a fixture of the human condition from which there is no escape. Or we can yield to the wish to pray or think it away.

The latter has an obvious psychological benefit but it comes at a considerable cost. We cannot satisfy the wish and still be human beings, if deep disappointment is more than a surmountable challenge. The alternative is to acknowledge our condition and refuse every picture of the world that makes it vanish through an act of cosmic wish fulfillment. This is what my mother did. It was the inspiration for her atheism, as I suspect it is for that of many of my friends.

But this is not the end of the matter. The Gods of Athens and Jerusalem are not compatible with an unyielding humanism. Is there some other God that is?

My mother thought no. My friends agree. The answer, I think, is yes. It is not the God of Athens or Jerusalem but a different and less familiar one—in certain respects, a hybrid of the two.

This novel God is not only consistent with the experience of deep disappointment. It alone makes this experience intelligible. Without promising relief from the peculiar sort of disappointment that separates us from all other animals, it also confirms the reality of a species of joy that is just as distinctively human. There can be no genuine humanism without it. We must now try to understand the nature of this unfamiliar God. When we do, we will see why those who say there is no God at all are as heedless of our humanity in one way as the philosophers and theologians who assure us that the phenomenon of deep disappointment is nothing lasting or real are in another.

4

Prospects of Joy

MY MOTHER EXPERIENCED a more or less average mix of happiness and loss. She divorced her first husband and out-lived two more. She was close to one of her sisters and es-tranged from the other. She loved her two boys, but under the shadow of her tormented belief that her own father, whom she adored, had never really loved her in return. On balance, though, my mother found life entirely worth living. She often said she was thrilled to be along for the ride.

Like most people, my mother took the durability of the world for granted. She found solace in the thought that her family and country would go on after she died. But she felt no need to be connected to anything eternal. She associated eter-nity with heaven and religion and God. She had no use for any of them.

Even the best people, my mother said, cannot look for-ward to a reward in heaven, or the worst to the tortures of hell. The world is all there is. One day, the small corner of the uni-verse we call home will no longer exist. One day, the universe itself will peter out in dark, cold night, to be reborn, perhaps, in a spasm of cosmic renewal—or perhaps not.

On and on things go, flickering and flying away, mocking the brevity and inconceivable smallness of our lives. A pandemonium of extinctions without end, the world contains no eternal order immune to death and destruction that might save the fleeting times of our lives from pointlessness and oblivion. Whatever meaning we discover in life we must find or make on our own.

After she died, I found among my mother's books a copy of Camus's *The Stranger.* In an afterword, the translator summarized Camus's view of life: "Though without purpose or meaning, life is the only thing that man has, the only reality he can know, and once he recognizes this and strips away his illusions he discovers that there is much in life he can enjoy and relish. . . . Camus places the full and terrible burden of living and dying upon the human being; he extends no hope of divine aid, of immortality; he makes each man responsible only to himself and to his fellow man for his acts and for his life. It is a grim, almost overwhelming burden, but Camus believes man is capable of shouldering it."[1]

In the margins, in the slanted hand I knew so well, my mother had written, "Great!"

She came to this view of life early on. As a young woman, my mother had already rejected the panaceas of religion that others in her family found consoling. She was an atheist long before she read Camus and Sartre and declared their existentialism to be her official philosophy of life. Camus's extravagant claim that immortality is an illusion, and the search for it an abdication of responsibility, merely expressed in grander terms a conclusion my mother had arrived at years before.

My mother was a highly intelligent person. But she was

not a trained philosopher. Her ideas were based on experience and avid if undisciplined reading. Many better-educated people, though, and not a small number of professional thinkers, share her view of life. Like her, they say they admire the courage to strive to make something meaningful of the short time we have, in the knowledge that there is nothing timeless to support our efforts, let alone guarantee their success.

Committed atheists who rail against organized religion fall into this group. They mock the belief that the meaning of life depends on our relation to an eternal God, who has the power to save us from the foolishness and disappointments of earthly existence.

Others take a more extreme position. They deny that the meaning of life depends on our connection to *any* eternal being or force, personal or impersonal. They are at war not just with the familiar God of the Abrahamic religions, but with the idea of eternity altogether. Those who cling to this idea, they say, are frightened children.

Many of my friends hold a version of this view, some more assertively than others. The obliteration of all the old institutions and practices that once gave eternity a presence in our lives creates the space for their atheism to flourish. It thrives in the ruins of the churches Philip Larkin loved to visit.[2]

Those who defend this point of view miss something important, however. In their zeal to rescue our humanity from a deforming reliance on the idea of eternity, they pass over the fact that among our goals there are some that we could reach only in an endless time, and whose attainment would require that we see the world from a point of view unconditioned by time altogether. That these goals are beyond our power to achieve is irrelevant. We can no more live without them than fulfill them. The result is that ours is a state of deep disappoint-

ment, lightened by the paradox that we are able to make progress even toward those goals that by definition lie beyond our
mortal reach.

This is the meaning of our most distinctively human pursuits. We need the ideas of timelessness and time everlasting
to explain them. Those who dismiss the idea of eternity as folly
or bad faith cannot account for the all-too-human mix of joy
and defeat that every pursuit of this kind entails.

The acknowledgment of the reality of this experience
leads to a further question. What must the world be like in
order to explain it? Our irrepressible curiosity moves us to ask.
We can never be content with the knowledge of who we are.
We want to know how the *world* must be arranged for it to be
possible for us to be who we are. Our longing to know will not
be satisfied until we have an answer.[3]

It cannot be the one the Abrahamic religions provide, for
on their view there is no unbridgeable gap between our longing for eternity and eventual attainment of it. Nor can the world
be as the greatest philosophers of pagan antiquity conceive it,
for on their view, too, eternity lies within reach. But this is only
a negative conclusion. It tells us what the world *cannot be like,*
so long as we refuse to treat the shortfall between our longing
for eternity and its fulfillment as a remediable error or forgiv-
able wrong.

Is there a positive answer to the question? Is there a picture of the world that explains how we can have such goals and
make progress toward them, though consummation remains
beyond reach? And if there is, how does it differ from the pictures that are such a familiar part of our cultural heritage—
those rooted in the venerable soil of Athens and Jerusalem?

The atheists and existentialists who share my mother's
dismissive view of God, and ridicule any suggestion that the
meaning of life depends on our connection to eternity, never

get as far as asking this question. They portray themselves as the champions of humanity, but their militant godlessness stops them from inquiring about the worldly conditions of the fusion of joyful progress and sure defeat that sets us apart from other living beings, whose ignorance of time rules out the experience of deep disappointment. It blocks the path that leads from anthropology to theology, which our longing to know compels us to follow.

If they pursued this path to the end, they would see that the human condition is explicable only on the assumption that the world is *inherently and infinitely divine.* They would understand that to account for our humanity, we must think of the world as what Spinoza calls the "face" of God.[4]

Modern science shows that this is so. So does romantic love. The intelligibility of every pursuit that is governed by a regulative ideal depends on Spinoza's conception of God. This is not a "saving" God, like those of Athens and Jerusalem. It cannot rescue us from our fate. But we need it to explain why we have the fate we do. For a humanist, this is something even better.

"It is owing to wonder," Aristotle says, "that men now begin and first began to philosophize."[5]

Wonder sparks curiosity but is not the same as it. My dog, Maisie, is curious. When we walk, she runs ahead, nosing her way. Her curiosity is active, like mine. It searches and probes. Wonder is by contrast receptive. It is alert yet passive. It is a kind of astonishment—a species of awe. It is the experience of being struck with amazement at the sheer fact that something exists.

As far as I can tell, my dog is never awestruck by the existence of anything, let alone that of the world as a whole. This is a peculiarly human experience. It leads to all sorts of further inquiries. But these are as distinctively human as the attitude of watchful amazement that gives them their start.

If we ask how wonder is possible, the answer is the one I have given before. We are detached from the world, in thought at least, and able to see it from a distance. We not only "suffer" or "undergo" time. We contemplate the flow of events from a position outside it. This enables us to imagine the enduring existence of things as something separate from their fleeting manifestations. And that, in turn, sets the stage for wonder. It makes it possible to be struck by the marvelous and mysterious fact that apart from their colors and shapes, their temperatures, tastes, and smells, the things we encounter in experience actually *exist*—to be arrested by the fact of their existence *as such*.

Human curiosity, like that of any animal, often has a practical motive. I want to know which of the berries I find on my walk are fit to eat. But to the extent it takes a distinctively human form, our curiosity is driven by a speculative interest in understanding the uncanny fact of existence itself.

Why do things exist? Why does the world as a whole exist? We value such knowledge for its own sake, apart from its material rewards. The desire to possess it is the impetus to all "pure" scientific research. There is nothing like this desire or the knowledge it seeks outside the astonished space of wonder.

The wonder that sets science in motion is immediately followed by another, equally wonderful experience. Amazingly, the world does not rebuff the questions we put to it—not completely, anyway. We need to put our questions carefully to get a meaningful reply. We have to conduct experiments to discover what we want to know. Still, the world is not a closed book written in indecipherable characters that the human mind can never grasp.

The idea of an experiment is as old as human curiosity. Today, it has reached unprecedented levels of sophistication.

Even our most ingenious experiments do not yield conclusive results. They only make some answers more probable than others. Further experimentation is always required. But the endlessness of our interrogation of nature, and the incompleteness of the answers we receive, should not blind us to the astonishing fact that the world gratifies our curiosity at all. This is the most wonderful thing we discover when our wonder at the existence of things prompts us to ask how and why they exist in the first place.[6]

The experience of the world's receptiveness to our wonder-struck desire to know is really two experiences at once. The first is that of an intelligible order we have not made up on our own. The experiments we devise to understand this order are clever human inventions. They are works of art. But the order they disclose, however incompletely, is not something we have created, too. It is not a fabrication. The answers that science yields have value only because the order they bring to light is independent of our curious minds.

The second experience is that of *resistance*. The world is not a closed book, but it is not an open one either. It gives up its secrets in bits and pieces and only under pressure. The reality of the world's intelligibility and its imperfect transparency are the wonderfully encouraging, and perennially frustrating, experiences of all who inquire into the reasons for the existence of things, motivated by their astonishment that there is a world at all.

These two experiences belong together. They cannot be disjoined. Nothing is more obvious. Yet nothing is more puzzling. How can the world be open to us but only imperfectly so? This has always been a question of philosophical interest. Modern science gives it added urgency. The progressive character of modern scientific research suggests that the world is *endlessly* open to us but *never* loses the opacity that frustrates our efforts to understand it. What must we assume about the world in order to explain the tension between these two experiences? I can see only one way to do so.

To account for the fact that the world becomes continually more comprehensible the further we test and probe it, we have to assume that there is nothing about the world we cannot possibly understand—that the world has an intelligible order, no part of which is permanently off-limits to our inquiring minds. At the same time, to explain why we can never completely grasp this order, we must assume that the intelligibility of the world is boundless and our minds severely constrained: that the first is infinite and the second finite, so that there can never be a final adjustment between the two. We are required to assume, in other words, that every question has an answer, that our storehouse of answers is forever increasing, but that an inexhaustible surplus of unanswered questions always remains.

There are many objections to this view; some are old and others new. I do not find them convincing.

Skeptics, for example, may ask how we know that the world has any order at all, let alone one we can understand. Perhaps we are just dreaming that it does. Perhaps an evil genius has given us this dream, along with the belief that it is true.

This was Descartes's thought experiment. He freed himself from its disturbing implications by a process of reasoning that some still find unpersuasive. In the end, he came back to the idea of an omnipotent creator as the guarantor of the objectivity of our beliefs (a weak reed on which to rest). A better response would have been to say that the experience of science itself is incompatible with such extravagant doubts, and that as between this experience, which is repeated all over the world every day, and the claims of a philosophical theory that denies it, the first will always prevail.[7]

Descartes was in fact not really dubious about the constructive work of modern science. He made many contributions to it himself. His skeptical challenge was launched from a philosophical position outside the actual practice of scientific research, with its continual reconfirmation of the reality of our discoveries together with the never-ending resistance the world puts up. Descartes's philosophical argument was made for the sake of putting this practice on a stronger foundation. It was a friendly challenge, sympathetic to science—one that implicitly acknowledged the authority of the experience it sought to justify and explain.

A more recent challenge comes from within the precincts of science itself.

The baffling discoveries of modern physics, and the theories that go along with them, have caused some scientists and laypeople to conclude that the world contains a residue of indeterminacy that can be observed and measured but never explained. At the deepest level, they say, the world is unknowably free. This is different from acknowledging that the complexities of the world are greater than we shall ever understand. It is a more radical claim. It denies that the world, at bottom, proceeds according to laws whose necessity makes them, in principle at least, intelligible to us.[8]

This is analogous to the old idea that the laws of nature have their origin in an act of divine will whose freedom puts it beyond the realm of necessity and therefore of all possible understanding. That idea has lost favor with many scientists. But in the minds of some, quantum mechanics has reinstalled a similar idea in the heartland of our most advanced understanding of the physical world itself.

The spontaneity they imagine at the root of things is that not of a purposeful will, but of a primal randomness instead (not unlike the process of random mutation that evolutionary biologists assume as a condition of natural selection). It is nothing like the personal freedom of the God of the Bible. But the implications for science are the same.

A law purports to define a necessary relation.[9] This is what makes it a law—even if only a hypothetical one. If the relation can be shown to be accidental, the law fails. It must be amended or abandoned completely.

If something happens spontaneously, then by definition it lacks the lawfulness that is the condition of all possible understanding. God's will used to be thought of in this way. Today, the "uncertainty principle" and the ideas of "superposition" and "de-coherence" are said by some to lead to a similar result.[10] They transfer the inexplicable freedom of a supernatural God to the innermost workings of nature itself.

These claims are hotly debated, in science and out. The technical details are forbiddingly complex. First-year college students can follow with relative ease Descartes's skeptical challenge to our belief in the reality of the world. The contention that the intelligibility of the world has an absolute limit because it arises from processes at the most elementary level, whose spontaneity makes them inaccessible to understanding, is by contrast extremely difficult for amateurs like me to understand, let alone assess.

Still, I am convinced that this view, too, must eventually yield, just as the earlier idea that God's will puts an absolute barrier in the way of our longing to understand the world in time gave way as well. That idea conflicted with the two-sided experience of modern science itself. The encounter with a world that opens itself to human inquiry, only gradually, partially, and obdurately, but without limit, is incompatible with the belief in a God whose freedom guarantees that the most basic fact about the world, on which our limited knowledge of every other fact depends, is in its essence strictly unknowable. The same experience is incompatible with the belief in a residual randomness that makes the universe as unintelligible at bottom as the doctrine of creation does at the top.

Of course one can say, "So much for experience." If a theory belies it, and the theory is compelling enough, the experience must yield to the theory. We have to resign ourselves to accepting the illusory nature of what our experience tells us is real. Few are ever likely to accept Descartes's philosophical argument that our idea of the world may be just a dream. But the claim that science itself has discovered an indeterminacy at the root of things that trumps our experience in a similar way today has wider appeal.

I remain unpersuaded. The whole of modern science rests on the expectation that further progress is always possible; that what seems inexplicable now will have an explanation later; that the limits that define our present understanding of the world will be superseded, to be replaced by others, and so on without end.

This expectation is more than strong. It is essential to the meaning and purposefulness of research in every field. This puts enormous pressure on all of us, scientists and nonscientists alike, to adjust our picture of the world to fit this expectation rather than abandon it on account of a theory, which, however plausible, demands that we reject the premise on which the vitality of modern science depends.

Many are proceeding on this premise, in the teeth of quantum mechanics and the principle of random mutation. They are searching for the cause of what has been said by some to be spontaneous and therefore beyond all understanding—which ceases to be so once its cause is found. Their goal is to explain what the science of the past century declares to be inexplicable. The debate over whether gravity better explains the "collapse" of alternative quantum states than the human act of observing them is an example. The revolution in molecular genetics is another.[11]

The results are as yet inconclusive (so far as I am able to judge). But those who are looking for explanations have science on their side. Their work sustains our encounter with a world whose order we are always able to grasp more fully than we do at present, yet never through and through. This is the original, ambivalent experience of wonder itself. No theory is strong enough to dispel or disprove it—neither those that purport to be the last word on the subject, nor those that claim to put an insurmountable roadblock in the way of deeper understanding.

To explain how this experience is possible at all, we are compelled to make two assumptions. The first is that the intelligibility of the world is an *inherent* feature of it and not an order imposed on the world by a transcendent God.

Aristotle held the former view and Newton the latter one. Newton gave the modern science of physics its first canonical formulation. His account of motion and inertia expressed in rigorous mathematical terms the new understanding of nature that replaced the Aristotelian picture of the world that had dominated Western science for centuries. But the laws of physics are all, Newton said, the gift of a God whose freedom is completely inscrutable. They owe their origin to an act of divine creation we can never understand.[12]

Newton's way of thinking traces everything we know about the world back to a supernatural power whose operations are strictly off-limits to human inquiry. Regarding all that happens in nature, it is appropriate to ask, "Why?" But if we misguidedly continue our inquiry and ask why God willed that nature have the order it does, the question is no longer one that calls for further research. We can make no meaningful progress in answering it. It has only the form of a question. Indeed, it is a question we *should not* even ask. It is a blasphemous or wicked question.

Every creationist theology has this stifling effect. It rests on a conception of divine freedom that permanently blocks the rationalizing vocation of scientific inquiry. The only way to remove the block is to assume that the intelligible order that science uncovers, patiently, layer by layer, is an inherent characteristic of the world and not the creation of God's unsearchable will. This was Einstein's view.[13] It is one of the two assumptions we have to make in order to account for the two-sided experience of wonder itself.

The second is that the intelligibility of the world is *infinite* as well as inherent.

Unlike Newton, Aristotle believed the world to be inherently intelligible. But he also assumed that its intelligibility is finite in nature—indeed, that it must be. Aristotle regarded the idea of the infinite as a stumbling block to reason, and he dismissed it on these grounds.[14] Only this guaranteed that deep disappointment is rationally inconceivable.

But Aristotle's assumption that the intelligible order of the world is bounded or finite is as incompatible with the program of modern science as Newton's belief that this order is due to the creative agency of a God who transcends the world altogether. If the latter frustrates our desire to know in a principled way, and converts the longing for complete understanding into a sin, the former wrongly suggests the longing can be fulfilled.

Consider the following example.

Last spring, I often saw a harrier hawk outside the window of my study on Block Island, flying low to the ground. I watched the hawk every day for several weeks. His movements intrigued me.

Why does the hawk fly as he does? I wondered. The answer seemed obvious. He was looking for mice and voles in the meadow across the road. He spotted them from above and swooped in for the kill. I saw it happen many times. But why does the hawk eat mice and voles, I asked myself, rather than seeds and grass, like the pheasants with which he shares the meadow? And why does he catch them by surprise from the air, rather than, say, creeping up on them as a fox might?

Aristotle believed that all these questions can be answered once I know what kind of bird the hawk is—once I grasp its nature. This takes time. I need to observe the hawk at work, doing its thing, on many occasions, before I can say with confidence that I recognize its ways. But once I have its nature "in mind," I know all that I need to know to understand everything that is understandable in the hawk's behavior.

There are other questions I might ask about the hawk, of course. Why did it fly past my window at nine in the morning on the first of March, and at ten a month later? Perhaps this had something to do with the lengthening day, and that in turn with the movement of the sun in the ecliptic, on its way to the summer solstice.

Why did the hawk sometimes swoop from west to east, but at other times from north to south? Perhaps this had something to do with the direction of the wind, and that in turn with the weather. Or perhaps it had something to do with the movements of the mice and voles in the field.

These are legitimate questions, and the answers to them can all be pursued, but, in Aristotle's view, only up to a point. Sooner or later, both questions and explanations run out. The latter depend on my knowledge of the different natures of things—of the hawk, the heavenly bodies, the elements that cause the weather, the natures of mice and voles. But not everything that happens can be explained in this way. Some things occur by accident. They are inexplicable. I cannot explain why a sudden gust of wind blows the hawk off course a second sooner rather than later, or the shadow of a passing cloud hides its prey from view at the exact moment it does.

Aristotle's world has an element of mindlessness in it. This lies beyond the power of a human or any mind to grasp. The residual mindlessness of the world is due, he thought, to the material dimension of things—to the ultimately unintelligible "stuff" in which every intelligible nature is embedded. We can get our "minds around" only the formal side of things. Their material aspect eludes all understanding.

If Aristotle's bounded cosmos, unlike Newton's infinite universe, is inherently intelligible, its intelligibility is confined by the distinction between form and matter that Aristotle took for granted. For Newton, absolutely everything in the universe runs according to God's plan. In this sense, the order of the world is limitless—though it is perverse to ask why the universe has the order it does. Aristotle thought this last question has an answer. But he also believed it is absurd to think that every question we can ask about the world has an answer too.

Anyone who thinks this shows that he is ignorant about the source and limits of the world's intelligibility. It is foolish, Aristotle says, to ask for more understanding than the forms or natures of things allow.[15] But the work of modern science rests on a foolishness of just this kind.

The regulative ideal that guides this work assumes that no question is absurd. Those who embrace it will never be satisfied by the response, "That was just an accident—there is nothing to explain it." Of course, we often accept this response as a practical matter. Life is too busy for us to stop and ponder every question we might. But the interminable program of modern scientific research, whose meaning and value we now all take for granted, assumes there is no question to which an answer cannot be found, if we pursue the matter far enough. That is because those who are today engaged in the endless campaign to understand the world do not think of it as being divided, in the way Aristotle supposed, between intelligible natures and unintelligible matter, or between individuals we perceive with our senses and ideas we conceive with our minds.

These divisions are conveniences of ours. We need them to meet the practical challenges of life. But they are not built into the order of things. The world is intelligible all the way down. There is an explanation for everything that happens, though we shall never do more than scratch the surface of what it is possible to know.

The intelligibility of the world is therefore not only intrinsic to it—contrary to what Newton supposed. It is infinitely deep—something Aristotle could not imagine. We need these two assumptions to explain the experience that human wonder brings to light, and modern science forever repeats, of a world whose order is unfenced by a divine decree that commands us to keep our knowledge within limits, yet never fully known by finite beings such as we.

There is one more assumption we need to make in order to explain the possibility of this experience. It follows from the other two. Many will think it implausible. Yet I find it the most compelling of all. It is the assumption that the world as a whole and everything in it are eternal and divine.

This is an unorthodox view. But it has advantages the more familiar theologies of Athens and Jerusalem lack. It offers a rational response to the existentialist dogma that nothing is eternal and the meaning of our lives unconnected to anything beyond time's solvent power. It enables us to explain the most characteristic features of modern life, in a way we cannot otherwise. And it accounts for the fact that our deep disappointment is accompanied by possibilities of joy that are uniquely human, too.

None of this brings the peace the Abrahamic religions promise or that final freedom from the cave of illusions that some philosophers hold out as the reward of thought. These are inhuman dreams. We should reject them. The assumption that the world is infinitely divine does not bring them back to life. But it has compensating advantages. It better explains the human condition than these deceptive portraits of it. It also offers a wiser answer to the ageless question of how we ought to live than those who say we must summon the courage to accept the fact that we are transient blips cut off from anything changeless and perfect.

The path that leads to my infinite God of the world starts from the simple idea of a law. I have discussed it before. I come back to it one last time.

I observe that my hawk is in the air an hour longer each day toward the end of March than he was at the beginning. I explain this change in his behavior on the ground that the lengthening period of daylight enables him to extend his forays over the meadow. This familiar way of speaking assumes a distinction between a "fact" to be explained, on the one hand, and the "ground" that explains it on the other. The fact is something specific. It is the particular event I observe (in this case, the flight of the hawk I watch from my study). The ground, by contrast, is general. It explains this fact and others like it—the similar behavior of other hawks that belong to the same species.

The generality of the reasons I offer to explain the event I observe is part of what I mean when I say that my explanation rests on a law. But that is not all. The concept of a law—of any law—has the idea of necessity built into it, too. A law says that one thing follows another for a *reason*. The law I have formulated regarding my hawk's extended flights does more than state that a change in its behavior follows a change in the length of the day. Into this simple declaration of succession, my proposed law inserts the little word *because*.

Without that, my law explains nothing. It is merely a register of observations. I begin to make the effort to account for what I see only when I assert that one thing does not merely succeed another as a matter of fact, but *must*, and therefore always will. Whether this claim can be sustained is irrelevant. No law derived from experience is insulated against disproof. What matters is the *meaning* of the claim itself. This is tied to the idea of necessity. Subtract that, and the notion of a law becomes empty. The attempt to explain anything at all falls to the ground.

A law is an abstraction. It inevitably leaves certain things out of account. The law that I construct to explain the duration of my hawk's flights says nothing about their speed, even though the hawk is always flying at a certain speed, sometimes faster, sometimes slower. It says nothing about the mood that I am in when I observe the hawk, though I am always in a mood of some kind—cheerful, morose, or distracted. My law omits these and countless other "irrelevant" factors. Their omission is essential to the law's explanatory power. Ignoring them is the price my explanation pays for the enlightenment it offers.

But my attention can shift at any moment to these omitted factors. I have explained, tentatively at least, why my hawk spends more time in the air as spring moves into summer. But why does it fly faster at some times than at others? I make a number of observations and construct a hypothesis to account for this, too. The hawk flies slowly when the wind is light and quickly when it is strong because the wind enables him to conserve his energy. Even my mood may become an object of inquiry, though the means of investigating it will be very different.

At every level, the same pattern reappears. Something I ignored before is now provisionally explained. But the law I propose to explain it also leaves many things out of account. It is an abstraction, too. I may have explained to my satisfaction why my hawk flies faster on windy days, but why does he fly at different speeds when the wind is blowing at the same one, from different directions? My law takes no notice of that. Yet I may become interested in this question, too, and pursue it with further observations, though these are likely to require a degree of precision I had not needed before. And so on, without end.

As I pursue these questions, I am slowly filling in the blank spots that every law includes just because it is an abstraction or generalization. I am constructing a net of laws whose weave is becoming finer and finer.

I know that I can never reach the end of this process. I also know that every law I propose, at every level of detail, is subject to disconfirmation in the light of further evidence. But the aspirational if unattainable goal of my increasingly subtle inquiries is an explanatory net so fine that it captures absolutely everything about the world—a system of laws so complete that it leaves nothing to be explained.

At this point (were it attainable), the distinction between fact and law would vanish. And because the very idea of a law implies the existence of a necessary connection among the things it purports to explain, the element of necessity that scientists strive to discover in the facts they observe would now have grown to encompass the whole of reality. There would be no inexplicable, "brute" facts left, only law, only necessity, down to the bottom of the world. An explanation of this kind lies beyond our power to achieve. But that does not diminish its power as an ideal.

Something even more astounding happens when we pursue our scientific investigations in an upward direction.

About every law one can ask, "What explains the application of this law within the range or sphere it purports to cover?" Why does the law I construct to explain the behavior of my hawk and others like it not apply to gophers and snails?

In this case, the answer can only be some higher-order law, of still greater abstraction, that accounts for the differences in animal behavior—perhaps something like Darwin's law of natural selection. Of course one can ask about this law, too, "What explains *it*?" The result is an upward-spiraling inquiry as endless as the downward one we follow into the bowels of the world.

There is a striking difference, though. The goal of our quest for ever-higher and more general laws would, could we finally reach it, still leave an important question unanswered. "Why is the world governed by *these* laws, rather than some *others*?" This is not a frivolous inquiry. There are scientists who have tried to explain even the most basic laws of physics as the result of an evolutionary process. Without these exact laws, they say, nothing in the universe could cohere for an instant (the analogue of reproductive success). A kind of cosmic anarchy would prevail.[16]

But this is not yet the end of our inquiries. One can press still further and ask why there is a world at all. "*Why is there something rather than nothing?*" This is the most elementary question the human mind can conceive. Beyond it, there is nothing further to ask.

So long as this question remains unanswered, our understanding of the world is more than incomplete. It is theoretically (though of course not practically) insecure. However far we have gone, in an upward and downward direction, in pursuit of explanations that account for what we find *in* the world, if the existence *of* the world itself remains a mysterious brute fact, all our knowledge rests on sand.

Those who believe in a God of Newton's sort have a ready answer. The world exists because God chose to create it. But this only shifts the inexplicability of the existence of the world to that of God's will. Our knowledge of everything in the world remains as groundless as before.

This undermines the entire enterprise of modern science at its foundation. Descartes was determined to avoid this result. In the end, he fell back, as Newton did, on the idea of an omnipotent but unknowable creator—a self-defeating strategy. To "save" the sense and purpose of scientific research, we have no choice but to assume (what Newton and Descartes denied) that the intelligibility of the world is an inherent feature of it. This alone explains why the limitlessness of the rationalizing ambitions of modern science is not a futile pretention. But if we make this assumption, what answer can we give to the question of why there is a world at all? So far as I can see, there is only one possible reply. It goes something like this.

"The world exists as a matter of fact. We have no reason to doubt its existence. But if the world *actually* exists, then it *must*. It cannot *not* be. That is because only the *necessity* of the world's existence can *explain* its existence as a matter of fact.

"If the world *might not* exist, there could be no account of why it does. Many, perhaps, are prepared to accept this conclusion. But no scientist can. Scientists explain facts by bringing them under laws. Every law asserts a necessary connection of some kind. If these all ultimately rest on a contingency for which there is no explanation, then the laws of science are not merely incomplete and provisional. They are not laws at all. The necessity of the connections they assert is a mirage. Science is a game—a will-o'-the-wisp. It is not the serious pursuit it claims to be.

"As scientists proceed to fill in the blanks of the world; to extend the web of explanation to cover all things, great and small; to convert facts into necessities by patiently chipping away at the distinction between abstraction and reality, they have no choice but to assume that the world exists by necessity. This is the only way to explain the fact that there is something rather than nothing compatibly with the ethos of modern science itself.

"If this most basic of all facts were inexplicable, not just for the moment in our present state of understanding, but permanently and in principle, then every other fact would be inexplicable, too. Others may reluctantly acknowledge or even enthusiastically embrace this conclusion. But those who love science cannot. To 'save the phenomenon' of modern research, with its insatiable demand for intelligibility, the practitioners, consumers, and admirers of modern science are driven to the breathtaking conclusion that the world cannot not be. No thought is further from our ordinary experience of things. Yet the work of science today demands it. Otherwise its efforts are pointless and vain."

I hear the laughter finally explode.

The Abrahamic religions have accustomed us to the idea that the existence of the world is a contingency, not a necessity. Even among disbelievers, the conviction remains strong that the world might not exist. It is the commonsense residue of the doctrine of creation. What could be more obvious? What is more absurd than the idea that the world cannot not be?

Yet once upon a time this idea seemed not only reasonable but inescapable. Aristotle, for one, enthusiastically embraced it. He arrived at it in roughly the way I have. Beginning with the phenomenon of human understanding, he wondered what must be true about the world itself for such understanding to be possible at all. This led him to a physics and then a metaphysics founded on the idea of a self-sustaining, self-actualizing cosmos that cannot not exist.

I am saying something similar. The experience of modern science is unthinkable except on the assumption that the world is inherently intelligible, and this in turn on the further assumption that it is impossible that the world not exist—the startling and strange conviction on which the prosaic work of scientific research now depends.

In one crucial respect, of course, my account differs fundamentally from Aristotle's. He did not believe that the world is *infinitely* intelligible. As a result, he saw no unbridgeable gap between what we yearn to know and what we can. His theology leaves no room for deep disappointment.

Aristotle was wrong. We live in a gap of this kind. Deep disappointment is the human condition. It arises from the chasm between the limitlessness of our ambitions and the finitude of the powers we have to pursue them.

Our ambitions are limitless because the intelligibility of the world itself has no limits. Modern science demands that we assume this. But if the existence of the world is intelligible only in case it *must* exist, and if the intelligibility of the world is infinite rather than bounded in the way Aristotle supposed, then not only must the world *as a whole* exist by necessity but everything in it—from the gaseous nebulae in the farthest reaches of the visible universe to the flea on my tip of my shoe—must exist by necessity, too.

Necessity is one way of thinking about eternity. Necessary states and relations are those that are unconditioned by time. If everything in the world, however large or small, durable or fleeting, is necessary, then everything is timeless or eternal in one sense of the word. The eternity of the world is coextensive with the whole of reality and not limited to the formal dimension of it, as Aristotle thought.

It would take an endless time for any finite being to fully comprehend this—an eternity in the second sense of the word. Aristotle was able cheerfully to affirm that a studious man can comprehend the necessity of the world's existence in the brief time before he dies, only because he assumed that the intelligibility of the world is finite, too.

Yet even when the task becomes an endless one that cannot be completed in any number of lifetimes, the goal remains the same. It is to understand the God of the world—a timeless and therefore everlasting God, though one that now exceeds all human understanding because it endows every crack and crevice of the world, every accident and seeming work of chance, with the same eternal being that is the essence of God's nature. This guarantees our deep disappointment. But it also explains it and accounts for the fact that we are able to make progress in the shadow of certain failure.

Lily Briscoe is a character in Virginia Woolf's novel *To the Lighthouse*. She has been struggling for years to complete a painting of the view from the summer house where the action of the novel takes place. Finally, she is done. "Yes, she thought, laying down her brush in extreme fatigue, I have had my vision." These are the last words of the book.[17]

I feel more than a little like Lily Briscoe. I have had my vision, too.

Most of the time the world looks to me, as it does to other people, like a parade of accidents and surprises. So much seems accidental that I sometimes wonder whether anything happens for a reason at all.

There is enough order in the world for me to get around—

to make plans (which sometimes fail) and pass judgments (which are frequently mistaken). But often in the past, and even now when my vision fails me, the world seems more chance than order. From time to time, if rarely, the thought still occurs to me that maturity is the acceptance of the irrationality of life, as we human beings experience it.

When the vision is upon me, though, I see these apprehensions in a different light. The experience of contingency then seems to me an inevitable consequence of the finitude of my perspective on the world. To call this an illusion is misleading. It suggests that I might overcome it if I tried. I cannot. That the world appears to me to be filled with inexplicable surprises is as real and incorrigible a phenomenon as the finitude from which it springs.

Yet even if I cannot overcome my finitude, I am consciously aware of it, in a way other animals are not. This puts me, in thought, beyond a limit I can never transgress in reality. I see with my mind's eye that there is something on the other side of the boundary my finitude erects. I long to understand it. What is the world really like, undistorted by what Spinoza calls my "mutilated" perceptions of it?[18]

This is not a question I can ever fully answer, nor can any succession of finite beings like myself. But I can make some modest progress on my own, and together we can make even more. There is no limit to what we are able to understand about the world as it really is.

I have come to see things as I do by asking what the world must be like for endless progress of this kind to be possible at all. I answer: The world can contain no brute facts, no pure accidents, as we casually assume it does, watching events unfold from our limited points of view. It must be wholly intelligible, from the smallest particle of reality up to its largest laws. It must exist by necessity; the world cannot *not* be.

My vision is not a private revelation—the gift of a loving God. It is not the afterglow of an intoxicated dream. It is as sober as the work of modern science, whose regulative ideal makes sense only on the assumption that the world is as I see it: one, whole, freestanding, infinitely intelligible, uncreated and unsustained by any power but its own.

This requires an adjustment in the way we think about the relation between science and religion.

Many view science as an antireligious force, perhaps the greatest of all. They see it as the enemy of faith and superstition —an engine of disenchantment. But this is true only if we understand religion in a narrow way.

In the broadest terms, religion has to do with God. This is how we define religion, in the West at least. Beliefs and practices are religious insofar as they are organized around the idea of God, in one version or another.

The idea of God in turn rests on the distinction between time and eternity. God is an eternal power or being that exists outside of time and therefore at every moment in it. This way of thinking about God is older than the religious traditions that shape the views of most people about God and religion today. The distinction between time and eternity lies at the root of every Western idea of God, from the Homeric (indeed, the Paleolithic) on. It explains the separation of God *from* the world, according to the Abrahamic religions, and defines the God *of* the world, in Aristotle's pagan theology.

The vision of the world that is needed to explain the work of modern science rests on the idea of eternity, too. It pictures the world as a timeless whole whose eternal nature can be grasped only in an eternity of time. This is not the God of the philosophers or prophets but a mash-up of the two.

The God of modern science is in the world, not beyond

it, as the prophets teach. More exactly, it *is* the world or, more exactly still, the intelligibility of the world.

The infinite intelligibility of the world guarantees that we shall never understand it completely. The Abrahamic critics of Aristotle's pagan rationalism were right to attack his belief that we can ever fully comprehend God with our human minds. But they were wrong to erect in place of his God one that converts our longing to know the eternal and divine, by means of reason alone and without any unaccountable help from God himself, into a regrettable temptation or sin.

The God of modern science restores God's eternal being from the supernatural realm, where the prophets placed it, to that of nature itself. Yet it preserves the idea of our distance from a God *beyond* the world and converts it into the permanent incompleteness of our encounter with the God *of* the world, as encoded in the regulative ideal that directs all scientific research today.[19]

The result is a God that looks like neither the familiar Abrahamic version of it, nor the pagan idea of divinity that the Abrahamic religions discredited once and for all. But it is a God nonetheless. It serves as the explanatory ground of everything that happens in time only because it is itself unconditioned by time.

Science needs this God to account for its own ideals. Those who think of God in Abrahamic terms, whether they are believers or disbelievers, imagine that devotion to God conflicts with or confines the boundless rationalizing impulse of modern science. The truth is just the opposite. The God of my vision gives this impulse sense and meaning.

The same is true of every pursuit that seeks a goal we can approach but never reach in time.

Romantic love is like this, too. Its goal is affection, not

disinterested understanding. It neither proceeds by laws nor seeks to discover them through an experimental process of testing and verification. But it also is defined by the hope, and episodic experience, of advancement in a work that can never be finished. And for some it is accompanied by the conviction that there can be no life or world without the love they feel— by a deepening sense of destiny that is an analogue of sorts to the idea of necessity that plays a more explicit role in the endless search for scientific knowledge.

Most important, romantic love is characterized by the same ambivalent experience of openness and opacity as that of the scientist who labors in the never fully occluded light of wonder. For those who accept the romantic ideal of love, which is as distinctively modern as its scientific counterpart, the experience of love is defined by the wonderful fact that love can always grow, and sometimes does, and by the equally impressive resistance it always encounters.

How can we make sense of this experience except on the assumption that the human being we long to love is infinitely lovable, though our powers of loving are all-too-obviously finite? And loveable not as a creature of God, whose worth springs from another source, but for his or her own sake?

Romantic love invites, indeed requires us to think of the beloved as inherently and infinitely lovable—like the inherently and infinitely intelligible object of scientific research. We all know how often the pursuit of this ideal fails. But this can never weaken its hold on our hearts—any more than our failure to live up to the ideals of science can loosen their grip on our minds.

This is the theology of romantic love. It draws on the ideas of timelessness and endless time and makes of them a new God, that of neither Athens nor Jerusalem, but a disenchanted fusion of the two. The experience of modern love depends on this idea of God to be intelligible at all. So does that of modern science. It alone explains the possibility of every human endeavor that aims at what can be enriched and strengthened over time but never fully finished in it. We need this God to account for the coincidence of disappointment and joy that defines the human condition, which the modern age has brought to light with liberating finality.

Contentment comes in countless forms and never lasts. There is the contentment of watching a child at play—of being a child at play. There is the contentment of a duty met, a job well done, an investment that pays returns. Contentment is woven through our lives, along with pain and loss. The only consolation for the fact that no contentment lasts is that no pain or loss does either.

Contentment is fulfillment. It is the experience of having completed or being completed by an activity of some kind. The contented person is at rest, for the time being at least, until the moment passes and life moves on.

Contentment exists only where completion is possible. The goal a contented person reaches must be within her grasp. She may fail to reach it. In that case, she will be disappointed. But things might have turned out otherwise. There is nothing about the nature of the goal itself that rules out the possibility of achieving it, and of experiencing the contentment this brings. Contentment is the other side of shallow disappointment.

Science and love are different. They are pursuits with no attainable end. Yet progress is still possible. Our understanding of the world deepens over time. We revise and discard old theories and substitute new ones for them. Sometimes our knowledge remains frozen for centuries. But on the whole, and in the long run, the direction of science is progressive. So is that of love, when it is flourishing and not moribund or repressed.

The experience that accompanies progress toward an unattainable goal is intensely gratifying. But it is not the experience of coming to rest. It seems, in fact, to be an experience of
the opposite kind: not of resting but of being in motion from
one condition to another—from a position of inferior understanding or deficient love to a more enlightened or affectionate
state.

The gratification this brings lasts only as long as the motion does. It ceases with achievement, unlike contentment,
which begins there. Or, rather, the contentment a scientist feels
when an experiment is successfully concluded, or a theory val-
idated by results in the field, is not only short-lived. It is antithetical to the spirit of science itself, which compels us to view
every achievement, no matter how grand, as a provisional resting place from which to gather strength and move on: a stag-
ing area, not a destination. Something like this is true of romantic love as well. Its fulfillments lie in the prospect of further
enrichment.

In this sense, contentment is false to the spirit of science
and love. But the gratification of advancing toward an unattainable goal is not. For this special kind of gratification, we
need a word other than *contentment*. Spinoza calls it *joy*.[20]

Joy, he says, is the experience of becoming more effective
in the use of a power we may successfully employ to different
degrees. This applies to powers of every kind—physical, intellectual, and emotional. We all possess these powers. None of
us can ever have as much of any of them as we want. Still, more
is better than less.

Each power is a potential. To the degree we realize it, we
ourselves become more real, and we all want, or should want,
to be as real as we can. Spinoza makes a similar point in response to those who say that unless virtue in this life is rewarded with eternal bliss in the next, we have no reason to be

virtuous at all. That is a childish attitude, he says. Even if we cannot have all the eternal life we desire, we ought to want to have as large a share as we can, and always more than we do at any moment.[21]

Without the idea of what is unconditioned by time, our longing to understand the world has no final goal. This gives science its purpose and direction. It provides the measure by which to judge whether we are making progress. It also assures disappointment. But at the same time it opens a space for the joyful experience of increasing power in the pursuit of an unattainable goal. The same is true of love. Love seeks what it can have only in an endless time. This makes disappointment inevitable, along with the prospect of continual advancement, until one's time is done.

To fall back, to be blocked, to be stuck in place in the endless campaign to know or love is the opposite of joy. Spinoza calls it *sadness*. Joy exists only in the moment of advance. It is, by its very nature, evanescent. Yet it buoys the spirit of those who experience it by filling them with the confident sense that, for the moment at least, they are actively working toward what lies beyond their reach.

Those who deny the possibility of deep disappointment are bound to think of joy in different terms. They can conceive it only as fulfillment—as the contentment of final arrival, an active state perhaps, but an active being-at-rest. This is how Aristotle imagines the perfect if not permanently sustainable condition of thought at which the wise man arrives in this life. It is how Dante imagines the happiness of the angelic choirs in heaven.

This is not the joy of research science or romantic love. Our regulative ideals put fulfillment beyond reach. But in doing so they guarantee that the experience of growing power—of power on the rise, full of hope for further progress, exuberant, alive—has no limit either, and grows as long as human beings continue to strive toward goals beyond their grasp.

The joy of science and love is the experience of drawing closer to the God of the world. Consummation is denied us. But we have the power to approach our goal, if we use the power wisely rather than neglect or abuse it. The joy this brings is not the remedy to deep disappointment. It is its correlate and companion. The intense if qualified rewards of joy are enough to make the pursuit worthwhile, even if they are not all we can imagine when, in our religious and philosophical fantasies, we dream our humanity away. They are in any case, as Spinoza wisely observes, the only rewards we have. And we alone, caught in time yet always looking beyond it, have even the chance to experience joy, which my contented dog, Maisie, is denied once and for all.

My vision has held me in its grip for twenty years. I have no wish to wrench myself free.

Some attack it fiercely. A few are believers who want to persuade me that their God is better than mine. Others are committed atheists who say we should refuse every idea of God, mine included.

Most of my friends, though, are simply bemused. They wonder why I am so attached to my ideas. To those who are curious, I try to explain my beliefs more clearly. It is never clear enough—for them or me.

I no longer think of my vision as a provisional hypothesis that I may upon reflection abandon. To me it is more a habitation than a hypothesis. It is where I live, and though (to continue the metaphor) I am constantly making additions and repairs, I have no expectation of moving to a new home.

My vision seems to me more humane than the alternatives. It credits the longing for eternity that religious men and

women regard as an obvious fact, without accepting, as they
do, that the longing can be fulfilled. It recognizes, as my existentialist friends are forever reminding me, that everything we
do and dream takes place in the stream of time that sweeps us
from birth to death, but denies that all our aspirations can be
defined in temporal terms. It does a better job of capturing the
special disappointment, and singular joy, that for better and
worse characterize our peculiar condition. It affirms a humanism that refuses to yield to illusions of fulfillment or nihilistic
bravado.

It also gives me a vantage point from which to organize
my thoughts about the tradition of Western philosophical
thought that I first began to explore fifty years ago. The more I
have read and reflected, the more convinced I have become
that this tradition is defined by the opposition between two
imaginative possibilities, those of Athens and Jerusalem. My
view of the human condition, and the vision of the world that
goes with it, has helped me understand what this opposition
means. It has helped me see what is distinctive about the ideals
of modern thought and how these differ from those both of
the ancient world and of the long Christian interlude that separates us from it. It has given me a way to think about the intellectual coherence of the civilization to which I belong.

Most important, though, my vision is fertile. It yields
insights wherever I look.

I have placed particular emphasis on the work of modern science because the strength of the vision seems especially
clear here. I have written about love to make the point that
it shapes even those experiences that seem furthest removed
from the impersonal precincts of science. But the power of the
vision hardly ends here. I see no limit to its reach. The excite-
ment of being in its grip these past twenty years has been, for
me, one of discovery—of the repeated experience of finding

that some new field of endeavor, some other branch of life, is most clearly seen in the light of my vision as well.

All my life, for example, I have been a reader of novels. They were the first serious books I read. *The Hardy Boys, The Yearling,* later *Tortilla Flat* and *Cannery Row*—these remain with me sixty years on. But it was only as a late adult that I began to wonder about the novel as a literary form. When were the first novels written? Who read them and why? How do novels differ from the epics and tragedies of classical literature?

Eventually, I found the clue I needed in a remark that Henry James makes in his preface to *The Portrait of a Lady.* A novelist, James says, creates a plot in order to illuminate his characters' individual temperaments. The plot provides the scaffolding needed to display their idiosyncrasies. The classical conception of the relation between plot and character is exactly the reverse. The characters in a tragedy are there only to make the plot vivid and arresting. The first exists for the sake of the second. Aristotle develops this idea in the *Poetics.*[22]

The difference between James and Aristotle might seem one of degree. But it is more fundamental than that. It reflects the same deepening interest in the uniqueness of human beings that defines the spirit of romantic love (the subject of so many novels).

Then, twenty years ago, I read Proust's *In Search of Lost Time.* Among other things, Proust's novel is a reflection on the purpose of writing novels. Late in the work, Proust's Narrator concludes that the novelist seeks to find and save the eternal in time: to translate our most fleeting experiences into images of undying beauty that rescue them from time's obliterating power. The novelist's work is never done. That would take an endless time. But it can be carried out with varying degrees of success, just as one can know and love more or less completely.[23]

Putting James and Proust together, I arrived at a view of

the form and purpose of the novel that fit my developing vision of life, or perhaps I should say reinforced it, for by this point every discovery I made seemed a fresh piece of evidence in support of my understanding of the human condition and belief in the unorthodox idea of God that is needed to explain it.

Something similar happened in my attempt to make sense of the history of Western painting, from the Renaissance on.

The spring before I began college, I took a course at UCLA on the history of art. I was thrilled by the images and fascinated by my teacher's account of the emergence of Renaissance art out of the spiritual world of the medieval icon painters, and the Mannerist, Baroque, Rococo, Academic, Impressionist, Cubist, and Abstract styles that followed. Was there an idea that explained this centuries-long development? Did it have a connecting theme?

I searched for an answer in the writings of the great art historians of the last century. Eventually, I concluded that the painters of the Renaissance transferred to their individual human subjects the infinite worth their Christian predecessors had assigned to the figure of Christ and the members of his Holy Family. I pursued this thought through the succession of styles that followed. Each now seemed to me an effort to depict more successfully than earlier styles had the eternal significance of some individual moment or personality. Constable expresses this goal when he says that his studies of clouds are meant to capture for all time the beauty of a single vanishing moment. I began to think of these works on canvas as the counterpart of Proust's work in words (as Proust himself did).[24]

This gave me a perspective from which to organize my reactions to the paintings I love and to understand my mixed feelings about some contemporary art. To say that this confirmed my vision puts it the wrong way round. The vision had by now grown so strong that it conditioned my perceptions and judgments about the works of literary and material beauty that I continue to enjoy—but with the added pleasure of encountering them in a frame of understanding that for me makes sense of life and the world as a whole.

Even my political ideals took a new direction.

I teach in an American law school. I consider myself a liberal democrat. My colleagues and I disagree about the meaning of these terms and the relation between them. But broadly speaking, we all subscribe to the ideals of liberal democracy. In the last two decades, though, my thinking about the ultimate meaning of these ideals has undergone a significant change.

Yes, it is essential that the rights of every citizen be protected. Yes, it is vital to secure the basic rules of democratic accountability. There are countless issues to explore here. But there is a further question beyond all these. What is liberal democracy *for*?

The answer that most appeals to me now is the one Walt Whitman gives in his essay *Democratic Vistas*. That rights are protected and the franchise secured are vital *preliminary* goods. But they are not the *highest* good. They are not the final end of democratic life. That is the creation of what Whitman calls an "idiocrasy"—a way of life that encourages the full flowering of every individual's unique personality, in a tapestry of infinite diversity that is the face of the God of the world to which we each make a singular and eternally meaningful contribution.

This last thought is the organizing theme of *Leaves of Grass*. It is a religious and poetic ideal. But it shapes Whitman's view of the ultimate goal of political life as well, as it now does mine. For me, too, our furthest democratic "vistas" lie in the range of religion. They make sense only in the light of my vision of the eternal and divine.[25]

Whitman wrote ecstatically in the grip of such a vision. It conditioned his view of everything, American democracy included. My experience has been the same—partly under Whitman's influence and partly as the result of reading Whitman's poetry from the vantage point of my own developing philosophical vision of things. I am too far gone for it to be otherwise.

For some of my friends, this is the sign of an obsession. Perhaps it is. I cannot say for sure that they are wrong. In any case, multiplying examples will not persuade them I am right. It can only illustrate how fertile I have found my vision to be.

There will always be more work to be done. I find the prospect joyful. This reflects my sense that the work is guided by a goal I can approach but never grasp, because it lies outside of time, while I am confined by it. Goals of this kind are a peculiar feature of the human condition. Even in our secular age, they remain as compelling as before. I know I have made many mistakes. I often get things wrong. But I know it is not a mistake to have such goals—any more than it is to be human.

Notes

Introduction

1. Mencken's account is hilarious and cruel. Few groups escaped his acid pen. He reserved his sharpest words, though, for the evangelical country folk of the "Bible belt"—a term Mencken himself appears to have coined. See Henry Louis Mencken, *A Religious Orgy in Tennessee: A Reporter's Account of the Scopes Monkey Trial* (Brooklyn: Melville House, 2006). Mencken refers to Dayton, Tennessee, as the "bright, shining, buckle of the Bible belt" in a July 15, 1925, dispatch titled "Law and Freedom, Mencken Discovers, Yield Place to Holy Writ in Rhea County." Ibid., 67–74. "The Hills of Zion" describes the scene outside the courtroom. See *Prejudices: Fifth Series* (New York: Alfred A. Knopf, 1926), 75–86. Mencken thought evangelical Christianity "the product of ill-informed, emotional and more or less pushing and oafish folk." "The National Letters," in *Prejudices: Second Series* (New York: Alfred A. Knopf, 1920), 38–39.

In Mencken's telling, evangelical Christians were convinced they could "claw into heaven" if they could just manage to "hate the Pope, to hate the Jews, to hate the scientists, to hate all foreigners, to hate whatever the cities yield to." "Protestantism in the Republic," in *Prejudices: Fifth Series*, 116. Of the "normal Americano" Mencken writes, "He is religious, but his religion is devoid of beauty and dignity." "On Being an American," in *Prejudices: Third Series* (New York: Alfred A. Knopf, 1922), 26. Yet though he found the theology unconvincing, Mencken thought "the poetry of Christianity is infinitely more beautiful than that of any other religion ever heard of." "The Poet and His Art," in *Prejudices: Third Series*, 169.

2. J. D. Salinger, "Down at the Dinghy," in *Nine Stories* (Boston: Little, Brown, 1953), 129.

3. Reform Judaism emerged from what David Sorkin calls the "religious Enlightenment" of the eighteenth century, which had a profound effect on Jewish as well as Catholic and Protestant thought. See David Sorkin, *The Religious Enlightenment* (Princeton: Princeton University Press, 2008). It attracted only a modest following in Europe but quickly grew to prominence in the United States. See Michael A. Meyer, *Response to Modernity: A History of the Reform Movement in Judaism* (Detroit: Wayne State University Press, 1995), esp. chap. 6, "America: The Reform Movement's Land of Promise." Today, more than a third of American Jews identify with the Reform movement—the single largest denomination. See "A Portrait of Jewish Americans," *Pew* (Oct. 1, 2013): 10.

From its beginning, the Hebrew Union College was known for its skeptical hostility to orthodox beliefs. The banquet held to honor the college's first graduating class exemplifies this attitude. It has come to be called the Trefa Banquet, a name that denotes the serving of non-kosher food, in this case clams and other shellfish, and dairy after meat courses. John J. Appel published the menu in "The Trefa Banquet," *Commentary* 41.2 (Feb. 1966): 75–78. He suggests the menu was not a mistake—the caterer was Jewish. In any case, the founder of the college, Rabbi Isaac M. Wise, though probably unaware of plans for the menu, turned the banquet "first into a test case of liberal convictions and gradually into an act of assertion of the 'new' Judaism," less concerned with *kashruth,* or dietary law. Ibid., 78. Samuel S. Cohon's "The History of the Hebrew Union College," *Publications of the American Jewish Historical Society* 40.1 (1950): 17–55, is a comprehensive history of the college from its founding in 1875 through 1950. See also "An Intimate Portrait of the Union of American Hebrew Congregations—A Centennial Documentary," *American Jewish Archives Journal* 25.1 (1973): 3–114; Lance J. Sussman, "The Myth of the Trefa Banquet: American Culinary Culture and the Radicalization of Food Policy in American Reform Judaism," *American Jewish Archives Journal* 57.1 (2005): 29–47.

4. Hiram Wesley Evans's 1926 essay, "The Klan's Fight for Americanism," offers a good portrait of the religious and cultural milieu into which my maternal grandmother was born a quarter century before. "The Klan's Fight for Americanism," *North American Review* 223 (March–May 1926): 33–63. The brand of Christianized Americanism that Evans defends is just what Mencken found so loathsome. See "On Being an American," 32 ("the Ku Klux Klan was, to all intents and purposes, simply the secular arm of the Methodist Church"), and the satirical "Contributions to the Study of Vulgar Psychology," in *Prejudices: Fourth Series* (New York: Alfred A. Knopf, 1924), 266–68.

1
The Humanist's God

1. My mother knew Sartre and Camus mostly from their literary works—in Sartre's case, *No Exit* (1944) (trans. Stuart Gilbert [New York: Vintage, 1989], 1–46) and *Nausea* (1938) (trans. Lloyd Alexander [New York: New Directions, 2013]), and in Camus's, *The Plague* (trans. Stuart Gilbert [New York: Vintage, (1947) 1991]) and *The Stranger* (trans. Stuart Gilbert [New York: Vintage, (1942) 1959]). She had also read Sartre's *Existentialism Is a Humanism* (trans. Philip Mairet [London: Methuen, (1946) 1973]) and Camus's *The Myth of Sisyphus* (trans. Justin O'Brien [New York: Vintage, (1942) 1955]), two readable statements of the core of their existentialist philosophy intended for a popular audience.

Being and Nothingness (1943) (trans. Hazel E. Barnes [New York: Washington Square Press, 1993]) is by contrast a work of forbidding difficulty. Sartre locates his argument in the tradition of transcendental phenomenology inaugurated by Edmund Husserl and carried forward by Martin Heidegger in *Being and Time* (trans. John Macquarrie and Edward Robinson [New York: Harper & Row, (1927) 1962]), to which the title of Sartre's own work makes more than oblique reference. Sartre is concerned throughout with the problems of self-knowledge and self-identity that Descartes put at the center of philosophical attention in the mid-seventeenth century. Some knowledge of these writers and their ideas is helpful if not required to appreciate the substance of Sartre's ideas.

2. The book is *Confessions of a Born-Again Pagan* (New Haven: Yale University Press, 2016). In it I approach the questions of this book from the top down rather than the bottom up. Here I begin with human experience—using my own as a guide—and work my way up to asking what must be true about the world itself in order for this experience to be intelligible at all. In *Confessions,* by contrast, I start with the great philosophical systems that have shaped our thinking about the nature of reality as a whole, from the beginning of the Western tradition to the modern age. Then, working down, I draw the implications of these highly abstract views of reality in general for the place of human beings within it.

I wrote this book in part because I felt the argument of my earlier one relied too heavily on a working knowledge of the history of Western philosophy. I wanted to convey in a more direct and less academic way some sense of the religious humanism that I would call my "philosophy of life." In the process, I discovered a range of questions I had not seen clearly before and arrived at a way of formulating them that I had not glimpsed. In this sense, writing this book has been for me a joyful experience, as I explain in the final chapter.

3. The point is vividly illustrated by Nevil Shute's 1957 novel, *On the Beach* (New York: Vintage, 2010). Shute's protagonists are the Australian survivors of a global nuclear war awaiting the arrival of the radiation cloud that will kill them and finish human life on earth. They still act decently, even courageously, and follow most of the same routines. But one of the essential conditions of a meaningful life has fallen away. The point of the novel is to remind us that life is meaningful only because we expect the world, or some part of it, to survive us.

4. Rilke expresses the thought with poetic grandeur. Even in the stars, he says, "time's transition glimmers." Rainier Maria Rilke, "Odd the words: 'while away the time,'" trans. Marielle Sutherland and Susan Ransom, in *Selected Poems* (Oxford: Oxford University Press, 2011), 129.

Hannah Arendt was particularly taken with this poem. She quotes it in "The Concept of History: Ancient and Modern," in *Between Past and Future: Eight Exercises in Political Thought* (New York: Penguin, [1968] 2006), 43. In the final chapter of *The Human Condition* (Chicago: University of Chicago Press, 1958), Arendt characterizes the modern age as one in which all the old durable structures of human life are increasingly consumed in a "process" of destruction and fresh invention that makes a mockery of the idea that anything survives time's all-destructive power (296, 300).

5. The most famous formulation is Nietzsche's in Paragraph 125 of *The Gay Science* ("The Madman"). "The madman jumped into their midst and pierced them with his eyes. 'Whither is God?' he cried; 'I will tell you. We have killed him—you and I. All of us are his murderers. But how did we do this? How could we drink up the sea? Who gave us the sponge to wipe away the entire horizon? What were we doing when we unchained this earth from its sun? Whither is it moving now? Whither are we moving? Away from all suns? Are we not plunging continually? Backward, sideward, forward, in all directions? Is there still any up or down? Are we not straying, as through an infinite nothing? Do we not feel the breath of empty space? Has it not become colder? Is not night continually closing in on us? Do we not need to light lanterns in the morning? Do we hear nothing as yet of the noise of the gravediggers who are burying God? Do we smell nothing as yet of the divine decomposition? Gods, too, decompose. God is dead. God remains dead. And we have killed him.'" Friedrich Nietzsche, *The Gay Science* (1882), trans. Walter Kaufmann (New York: Vintage, 1974), 181.

Thirty-five years later, in 1917, Max Weber gave a celebrated public lecture in which he took up the Madman's theme in more measured tones. "Science as a Vocation," trans. Hans A. Gerth and C. Wright Mills, in *From Max Weber: Essays in Sociology* (Abingdon, U.K.: Routledge, [1946] 1991), 129–56. "The fate of our times," Weber writes at the end of the lecture, "is characterized by the rationalization and intellectualization and above all by the disenchant-ment of the world. Precisely the ultimate and most sublime values have re-treated from public life either into the transcendental realm of mystical life or into the brotherliness of direct and personal human relations." Ibid., 155. Weber refers to Nietzsche only once, but the philosopher's spirit hovers over the lecture from its prosaic beginning to its prophetic end.

More recently, Charles Taylor has explored the historical and philosoph-ical meaning of the phenomenon of disenchantment in immense detail in *A Secular Age* (Cambridge: Belknap Press of Harvard University Press, 2007). Many still believe in God, Taylor says, but belief is now an "option." In Tay-lor's view, disenchantment is the name we give to the complex process, both practical and intellectual, through which, over the past half millennium, God's eternal presence ceased to be an objective reality and became a spiri-tual preference instead. Taylor is a devoted Catholic. His diagnosis of the process of disenchantment prepares the way for a deeply felt and rigorously thoughtful examination of the possibilities for the restoration of theism in our secular age—one whose ambition I admire but whose conclusions I reject.

6. Freud's classical account of religion as a neurotic disorder expresses what, for many today, has become a conventional truth. *The Future of an Il-lusion,* in *The Standard Edition of the Complete Psychological Works of Sig-mund Freud,* ed. and trans. James Strachey, vol. 21 (New York: W. W. Norton, 1961). Freud is often viewed as a foe of religion. If one understands religion in theistic terms, especially those we associate with the Abrahamic religions, there can be no question that Freud's relentless rationalism made him hos-tile to what he considered the self-imposed blindness of religious belief (the essence of every neurosis).

Whether Freud's rationalism itself has a spiritual dimension is a more complicated question. I believe that it does. The "theology" of psychoanaly-sis is the *Ethics* of Spinoza, to whom Freud referred with admiration. Freud's devotion to reason, his acceptance of the human condition as one of deep disappointment, and his confidence in the possibility of endless if never complete progress toward self-understanding are among the inspirations for the view of life I offer in these pages. I have more to say about Freud and his Spinozism in *Confessions of a Born-Again Pagan, 702–54.*

7. Montaigne's philosophy is deliciously complex. He weaves different themes depending on his mood. He is by turns a skeptic, a relativist, an in-trospective connoisseur of his own inner life, an exemplary "vivisectionist" of the soul, to use Nietzsche's phrase. See Friedrich Nietzsche, *On the Gene-alogy of Morals,* trans. Walter Kaufmann (New York: Vintage, [1967] 1989), 101. In "On Experience," Montaigne stresses the connection between the

brevity of life and the meaning of what we make of it. "It takes management to enjoy life," he writes. "I enjoy it twice as much as others, for the measure of enjoyment depends on the greater or lesser attention that we lend it. Especially at this moment, when I perceive that mine is so brief in time, I try to increase it in weight; I try to arrest the speed of its flight by the speed with which I grasp it, and to compensate for the haste of its ebb by my vigor in using it. The shorter my possession of life, the deeper and fuller I must make it." Michel de Montaigne, "Of Experience," in *Montaigne's Essays and Selected Writings: A Bilingual Edition*, trans. Donald M. Frame (London: St. Martin's Press, 1963), 447. This view of life was encouraged in part by the writings of the ancient Stoics and Epicureans, and by those of Lucretius in particular, whose rediscovery in the fifteenth century had an immediate and far-reaching effect. (In *The Swerve* [New York: W. W. Norton, 2011], Steven Greenblatt tells the story with a novelist's flair.) There was, though, one crucial difference between Montaigne's situation and that of Lucretius, writing in the first century before Christ. Life may be fleeting and the present order of the world only passing, as Lucretius claimed, but he still believed in the existence of gods living "between" the worlds and watching their succession from a vantage point beyond it. This Archimedean point was no longer available to the philosophers of an increasingly irreligious age.

Hume's views are famously recorded in a deathbed conversation with James Boswell. Boswell had gone to visit the dying philosopher. He wondered whether, on the verge of death, Hume had changed his mind about the prospects of a future existence. It is a question reminiscent of the one Socrates' students put to him the evening before his execution. See Plato, *Phaedo*, trans. Harold North Fowler, Loeb Classical Library 36 (Cambridge: Harvard University Press, 1966), 63b. "I had a strong curiosity to be satisfied," Boswell writes, if Hume "persisted in disbelieving a future state even when he had death before his eyes. I was persuaded from what he now said, and from his manner of saying it, that he did persist. I asked him if it was not possible that there might be a future state. He answered it was possible that a piece of coal put upon the fire would not burn; and he added that it was a most unreasonable fancy that we should exist for ever." Boswell persisted. "I asked him if the thought of annihilation never gave him any uneasiness. He said not the least; no more than the thought that he had not been, as Lucretius observes." James Boswell, "An Account of My Last Interview with David Hume, March 3, 1777," in *The Enlightenment: A Comprehensive Anthology*, ed. Peter Gay, vol. 2 (New York: Simon and Schuster, 1973), 265. While he lived, Hume cared quite a bit about the reception of his ideas and his reputation as a philosopher. But the meaning of life was for him wholly detached from the belief in any kind of individual immortality, which he considered a baseless superstition.

8. Martin Hägglund, *This Life: Secular Faith and Spiritual Freedom* (New York: Penguin Random House, 2019). Hägglund develops his argument by reminding the reader of the ways in which our intimate relationships and personal projects would lose their meaning if we had an endless time to pursue or enjoy them. There is truth in what he says. It is not, however, the whole truth. Yes, it is impossible to imagine love, or any project for that matter, retaining its human character if transposed to a state or condition where time never ends and therefore never passes. If the dream of endless love could be fulfilled, it would no longer be human love at all. This is a powerful point. Others have made it, too. See Bernard Williams, "The Makropulos Case: Reflections on the Tedium of Immortality," in *Problems of the Self* (Cambridge: Cambridge University Press, 1973), 82–100. But it overlooks the fact that although the fulfillment of the longing for an endless time in which to do and be all we can would mean the end of the human condition, the longing itself and the prospect of moving ever closer to its fulfillment are a part of the human condition, too. If fulfillment means its end, so would the erasure of the longing (neither of which is possible, so long as we continue to be human at all).

It is striking that in his moving and profoundly thoughtful meditation on the human condition, Hägglund has little to say about science, on which I place great weight in my own argument. One might even say that I interpret the meaning of love (which Hägglund places at the center of his account) in light of that of science. My reason for adopting this strategy is that the role of regulative ideals, which express the pathos and joy of the human condition with special clarity, is more prominent in the work of scientific research, though, as I attempt to show, it is equally important to understanding the meaning of love as we experience it today.

9. In his "Letter on Humanism," written shortly after the end of the Second World War, Martin Heidegger remarks that "of all the beings that are, presumably the most difficult to think about are living creatures, because on the one hand they are in a certain way most closely akin to us, and on the other are at the same time separated from our ek-sistent essence by an abyss." "Letter on Humanism" (1946–47), trans. Frank A. Capuzzi and J. Glenn Gray, in *Basic Writings*, ed. David Farrell Krell (San Francisco: HarperSan-Francisco, 1977), 230. Seventeen years earlier, in a lecture course titled "Fundamental Concepts of Metaphysics" (1929–30), Heidegger had described animals as "poor in world." Heidegger, *The Fundamental Concepts of Metaphysics*, trans. William McNeill and Nicholas Walker (Bloomington: Indiana University Press, 1995), 186.

For Heidegger, the difference between human beings and nonhuman animals is that we not only die but live "toward death." Death is for us not an event we experience, in the way we do other events in the course of our lives. It is the anticipated terminus of all our experiences and, as such, casts its shadow back over our lives as a whole. Our awareness of mortality transforms the meaning of everything we do, even our most prosaic experiences. Heidegger calls our foreknowledge of death "ecstatic." Only a being who "stands out" from the current of time is able to grasp it as an object of thought and to see his or her place in it as one who comes into being and passes away. Transcendence and time-consciousness are for Heidegger nearly identical concepts. They are closely linked even in his early writings. *Basic Problems of Phenomenology* (1927), trans. Albert Hofstadter (Bloomington: Indiana University Press, 1982), explores the connection in a particularly lucid way.

Our ecstatic knowledge of death remained for Heidegger the mark of our separation from all other animals and the key to understanding, among other phenomena, the experience of "having" a world as opposed to merely inhabiting one. *Basic Problems* is of particular interest in this connection. It presents in clearer terms many of the themes of Heidegger's better-known and nearly contemporaneous work, *Being and Time* (1927), trans. John Macquarrie and Edward Robinson (New York: Harper & Row, 1962). It also shows how Heidegger's understanding of human time-consciousness was shaped by his reading of Kant's *Critique of Pure Reason* (1781), trans. Paul Guyer and Alan W. Wood (Cambridge: Cambridge University Press, 1982), the fruits of which are more fully contained in *Kant and the Problem of Metaphysics*, trans. Richard Taft (Bloomington: Indiana University Press, 1990), also written in the crucial years 1927–28.

10. Kant, *Critique of Pure Reason*, Bxxxii.

11. The phrase appears in Aristotle's essay on the phenomenon of life, the treatise that has come down to us under its Latin title *De Anima*, trans. J. A. Smith, in *The Works of Aristotle*, ed. W. D. Ross, vol. 3 (Oxford: Clarendon Press, 1931), 415b. I discuss the passage in which it appears at greater length in chapter 3.

2

Endless Time

1. John Ruskin, "The Nature of the Gothic," in *The Works of John Ruskin*, ed. E. T. Cook and Alexander Wedderburn, 39 vols. (London: George Allen, 1903–12), 10:245. To a reader today, the most surprising thing about Ruskin is his preference for Gothic forms over their Renaissance successors. Ruskin associated the Gothic style with an attitude of reverence that was displaced

by the prideful spirit of the Renaissance, which placed the human being in the position of supreme value that before had been occupied by God, and subjected the work of art to rational control. This is particularly clear in Ruskin's three-volume *The Stones of Venice,* which Ruskin said had "no other aim than to show that the Gothic architecture of Venice had arisen out of, and indicated in all its features, a state of pure national faith, and of domestic virtue; and that its Renaissance architecture had arisen out of, and in all its features indicated, a state of concealed national infidelity, and of domestic corruption." "The Crown of Wild Olive" in *The Works of John Ruskin,* 18:443. For Ruskin, the architectural forms of the Renaissance indicate a moral decay, the result of pride, which encompasses "Pride of Science, Pride of State, and Pride of System," and "Infidelity," which included a new "respect for Paganism" and "the corruption of Catholicism." *The Stones of Venice,* vol. 3, in *The Works of John Ruskin,* 11:46, 121. In contrast, "humility . . . is the very life of the Gothic school." *The Stones of Venice,* vol. 2, in *The Works of John Ruskin,* 10:244. This was particularly evident to Ruskin in the typical Gothic accumulation of decorations made by anonymous craftsmen over centuries of collective effort.

2. Alexander Pope, *An Essay on Man,* ed. Tom Jones (Princeton: Princeton University Press, 2016), III.72.

3. Some philosophers refer to the knowledge of existing in time, as distinct from the mere fact of doing so, as time-consciousness. A great deal has been written on the subject. Edmund Husserl treats it at length in *The Phenomenology of Internal Time-Consciousness,* trans. James S. Churchill and ed. Martin Heidegger (Bloomington: Indiana University Press, 1964). It is also a central theme in Heidegger's *Being and Time.* My own understanding of the phenomenon and of its implications for the distinctive character of human experience in general has been shaped by Kant's profound discussion of it in the *Critique of Pure Reason* (1781), trans. Paul Guyer and Alan W. Wood (Cambridge: Cambridge University Press, 1982).

There are different ways to approach this epoch-making work. The most familiar is as a work of epistemology, a study of the grounds and limits of human knowledge. There is, however, another way to read it—as an answer to the question of what it means to be a human being. Human beings differ in so many ways, culturally and historically, that this question may seem impossible to answer, absurd even to ask. Is there anything about the experience of being human that remains constant across this immensely varied terrain? Kant was convinced there is. The phenomenon of time-consciousness is the key to his answer. Nowhere is this clearer than in the section titled "On the Schematism of the Pure Concepts of the Understanding" (*Critique of Pure Reason,* A137/B176). This way of reading Kant's *Critique* has long seemed compelling to me. My thinking was first turned in this direction by Heidegger's two brilliant commentaries on the work, *Kant and the Problem of Metaphysics*, trans. Richard Taft (Bloomington: Indiana University Press, 1990), and *What Is a Thing?*, trans. W. B. Barton and Vera Deutsch (Chicago: H. Regnery, 1967).

4. Friedrich Nietzsche, *The Birth of Tragedy*, trans. Ian Johnston (Arlington, Va.: Richer Resources, 2009), 29. The relation of time to eternity is one of the most challenging themes in Nietzsche's writings. At many points he characterizes the idea of eternity as the refuge of those afraid of life and unwilling or unable to live it on its own terms. He describes the invention of the idea as a strategy of revenge. See, for example, his famous discussion of ascetic ideals in the last section of *On the Genealogy of Morals*, trans. Walter Kaufmann (New York: Vintage, [1967] 1989), 97–164, and his portrait of Socrates in *Twilight of the Idols*, trans. Duncan Large (Oxford: Oxford University Press, 1998), 11–15.

Yet Nietzsche also believed that with no connection to eternity, what happens in time has no meaning. In place of the old, discredited but still authoritative Christian idea of eternity that in Nietzsche's view hovers over the modern world like an impotent ghost, he sought to erect a new idea that would restore meaning to time and save the world from nihilism, without relying on a God beyond the world to do so. This is one of the meanings of his remarkably beautiful if obscure teaching regarding "The Eternal Recurrence of the Same." See *The Gay Science* (1882), trans. Walter Kaufmann (New York: Vintage, 1974), 230, 273, and *Thus Spoke Zarathustra*, ed. Robert Pippin and trans. Adrian Del Caro (Cambridge: Cambridge University Press, 2006), 178.

5. The phenomenon of neurosis is the starting point of Freud's theory of psychoanalysis. Only we can be neurotic. We all are to some degree. Other animals are not. This is one reason we sometimes envy their relaxed enjoyment of sex though we would never trade places with them. It is also the reason we need a special sort of therapy for the neuroses that bedevil our lives. That they do is a consequence of the fact that we invest our longings—above all, those of an erotic kind—with a meaning no animal does. We yearn not just for orgasmic release but the fulfillment of love, whose hopes and fears are inseparable from the knowledge of death. As a result, our erotic lives are more than a succession of conquests and disappointments. They are organized around fantasies that carry us in imagination beyond any satisfaction that sex alone can ever offer. Freud's early attempts to understand the phenomenon of hysteria first brought this feature of our humanity into clinical view. See *Dora: Fragments of an Analysis of a Case of Hysteria*, in *The Standard Edition of the Complete Psychological Works of Sigmund Freud*, ed. and trans. James Strachey, vol. 7 (New York: W. W. Norton, 1961).

6. Johann Wolfgang von Goethe, "Toward a Theory of Weather," in *Goethe: The Collected Works,* vol. 12, *Scientific Studies,* ed. and trans. Douglas Miller (Princeton: Princeton University Press, 1995), 146. David Hume says something similar: "The winds, rain, clouds and other variations of the weather are supposed to be governed by steady principles; though not easily discoverable by human sagacity and enquiry." *An Enquiry Concerning Human Understanding,* ed. L. A. Selby-Bigge and P. H. Nidditch (Oxford: Clarendon Press, 1975), 88.

7. Aristotle, *Meteorologica,* trans. H. D. P. Lee, Loeb Classical Library 397 (Cambridge: Harvard University Press, 1952). The weather presented a special challenge for Aristotle. Rain, clouds, wind, and the like result from the cyclical movement of the elements returning to their proper place in the world. They exhibit the same permanence-in-change as all terrestrial phenomena, most strikingly the ever-circling life of plants and animals. The heavenly bodies show this too, though in their case change is limited to change of place. The planets and stars remain forever the individual beings they are (unlike plants and animals). But some celestial phenomena show a mutability that makes them more like rain and clouds than the sun or moon. Meteors and comets fall into this category. Aristotle included these phenomena in those to be explained by the principles of meteorology (hence the name of the science). But this implied a violation of the distinction between terrestrial and celestial motion that was fundamental for Aristotle. Hence the special challenge.

8. Martin Luther King Jr., "I Have a Dream," in *A Testament of Hope: The Essential Writings of Martin Luther King, Jr.,* ed. James Melvin Washington (San Francisco: Harper and Row, 1986), 217–20.

9. William Shakespeare, "Sonnet 116," in *The Sonnets,* ed. G. Blakemore Evans (Cambridge: Cambridge University Press, 1996), 90.

10. Kant introduces the concept of a regulative principle and discusses it at length in the *Critique of Pure Reason,* A508/B536–A567/B595. On the one hand, Kant insists that all human experience is limited or finite. The objects of experience are given to us. We do not invent or create the world itself. Further, our experience of the world is unavoidably temporal. Every experience we have belongs to a successive series of such experiences, each linked to those before and after it. The givenness of the world and the temporality of our experience of it are the defining marks of the finitude of the human condition. On the other hand, though we can never grasp the world as it is in itself, or experience it outside the framework of time, we are able to form the idea of a being or thing whose existence is not temporally confined. The most familiar example is the idea of God. The idea of a world that exists by necessity, and therefore eternally, falls into the same category, as does the

idea of ourselves as beings with eternal souls invulnerable to time. We can never experience any of these things. The debate over their existence is purely speculative and therefore interminable. One of the lessons of the *Critique of Pure Reason* is that our finitude rules out forever any final resolution of these perennial quarrels.

Yet the same ideas, though they refer to what can never be apprehended in time, direct our experience over time toward a richer and more adequate, though always incomplete, fulfillment of our two most basic longings: to live up to our responsibilities as moral beings and to satisfy our curiosity as thinking ones. In each case, we are able to make progress, guided by an ideal we can approach but never reach.

Kant discusses the first in the *Critique of Practical Reason*. What he there calls the two "pure postulates" of practical reason—the assumption that the world has an author outside of time and that our souls are immortal—inspire and direct our efforts to mold the world so that (as Kant puts it) every human being eventually receives the measure of happiness he or she deserves—an endless project of reform. *Critique of Practical Reason*, in *Practical Philosophy*, ed. and trans. Mary J. Gregor (Cambridge: Cambridge University Press, 1996), 246.

He takes up the second in the *Critique of the Power of Judgment*. In his discussion of what today we call research science, Kant maintains that the idea of an omnipotent creator outside of time is required to explain the possibility of the progress of scientific research, over time, toward an ever-greater but always incomplete comprehension of the timeless system of laws that it seeks to grasp. *Critique of the Power of Judgment*, trans. Paul Guyer and Eric Matthews (Cambridge: Cambridge University Press, 2000), 268–69.

The concept of a regulative principle is the key to understanding the connections among all three of Kant's "critiques" and therefore the unity of his critical system as a whole. I employ the concept here, though without the specifically Christian assumptions that for Kant still undergird it.

11. Nowhere is this thought expressed more simply than in the opening sentence of the preface to the first edition of Kant's *Critique of Pure Reason*. "Human reason," Kant writes, "has the peculiar fate in one species of its cognitions that it is burdened with questions which it cannot dismiss, since they are given to it as problems by the nature of reason itself, but which it also cannot answer, since they transcend every capacity of human reason." *Critique of Pure Reason*, Avii.

12. Plato in particular was deeply impressed by the familiar yet remarkable experience of grasping a mathematical truth. It served for him as the model of all knowledge in general. For Plato, every really real thing possesses the kind of eternity that mathematical truths do. It exists of necessity. It can-

not not be. This is the defining characteristic of what Plato calls the "Forms" of things, as opposed to their fleeting appearances in the realm of time, of "coming to be and passing away." *Republic*, trans. Paul Shorey, in *Collected Dialogues of Plato*, ed. Edith Hamilton and Huntington Cairns (Princeton: Princeton University Press, 1980), 485a–b. Nowhere in Plato's writings is the force of mathematics more vividly displayed than in the *Meno*, where Socrates helps a slave boy with no education understand a geometrical proof that even most well-educated readers initially have trouble following. *Meno*, trans. W. K. C. Guthrie, in *Collected Dialogues of Plato*, 82b–85c.

13. Hume, for example, distinguishes between "relations of ideas" and "matters of fact." "Of the first kind," he says, "are the sciences of geometry, algebra and arithmetic." Their truths are necessary. They can be shown to be true "by the mere operation of thought, without dependence on what is anywhere existent in the universe." Matters of fact, by contrast, are contingent. "The contrary of every matter of fact is still possible." Their truth can never be demonstrated by reason alone. Only experience brings them to light, and their truth is always subject to revision or disconfirmation in the light of further experience. *An Enquiry Concerning Human Understanding*, 25. Hume's distinction is widely accepted today. It is axiomatic in much of the modern philosophy of science.

14. In contrast to Plato, Aristotle made fundamental contributions to every branch of science. He gave lectures on what today we call physics, biology, psychology, astronomy, and meteorology, among other disciplines. His writings continued to shape the direction of scientific thought up to the threshold of the modern age, whose new science was born in part of a reaction to Aristotle's. In the West, the influence of Aristotle's scientific writings, largely dormant for the first millennium of the Christian era, grew enormously after the reappearance of his texts in Arabic translations that had already existed for some time. Aristotle was not only a scientist, though. He was what we now call a philosopher of science. He reflected on the metaphysical assumptions underlying the different branches of scientific inquiry, organized these in a systematic fashion, and formulated them in terms that also remained canonical for centuries.

15. Aristotle, *Metaphysics*, trans. Hugh Tredennick (Cambridge: Harvard University Press, 1933), 980a 22. Jonathan Lear offers a wonderful account of the implications of this one simple idea for the whole of Aristotle's philosophy. It is as fine a guide as I know to the system of Aristotelian thought in general. Lear, *Aristotle: The Desire to Understand* (Cambridge: Cambridge University Press, 1988).

16. The literature on the subject is immense. Karl Popper is generally credited with formulating the principle of falsifiability as a rule of scientific

inquiry. *The Logic of Scientific Discovery* (Abingdon, U.K.: Routledge, [1959] 2002), 17–20, 57–73. For further discussion, see critical work by Popper's protégé Imre Lakatos, especially "Science and Pseudoscience," in *The Methodology of Scientific Research Programmes*, ed. John Worrall and Gregory Currie (Cambridge: Cambridge University Press, 1978). Lawrence A. Boland applies the principle to economics in *The Foundations of Economic Method: A Popperian Perspective*, 2nd ed. (London: Routledge, 2003); Thomas Trzyna applies it to literature in *Karl Popper and Literary Theory* (Leiden: Brill Nijhoff, 2017). Thomas Kuhn develops the obverse of Popper's formula in *The Structure of Scientific Revolutions*, 4th ed. (Chicago: University of Chicago Press, 2012), 144–46. Malachi Haim Hacohen's *Karl Popper, the Formative Years, 1902–1945: Politics and Philosophy in Interwar Vienna* (Cambridge: Cambridge University Press, 2000) traces the development of Popper's thinking regarding the principle of falsifiability.

17. Hume elegantly states his view in section IV of *An Enquiry Concerning Human Understanding*. It can also be found in his *Treatise of Human Nature*, ed. L. A. Selby-Bigge and P. H. Nidditch (Oxford: Clarendon Press, 1978), 82–94. Hume's full position is complex. Though denying that we can ever have a knowledge of causes, he maintains (1) that our understanding of the connections among things improves over time (*Enquiry*, section VI); (2) that the idea of a cause entails that of necessity (section VIII); and (3) that we cannot conceive of nature except as a causally ordered whole from which "chance" is entirely absent (section VI). We must assume, Hume says, that "many secret powers lurk" in the world (section VIII), though we do not and never can know them except through their outward appearances, from which we are never entitled to draw the conclusion that one thing is caused, that is, necessarily determined by, another—a conclusion that is perfectly legitimate when considering mathematical truths. In these respects, Hume's position, as I interpret it, is closer to Kant's and to mine than is sometimes acknowledged. But interpretations differ. I admit to reading Hume in the hindsight of Kant's reply to him.

18. John Rawls, *A Theory of Justice* (Cambridge: Belknap Press of Harvard University Press, [1971] 2005), 587. The tradition of contractarian political philosophy to which Rawls belongs exemplifies the point more generally. Hobbes, Locke, and Kant construct their arguments by first assuming a pre-political condition, which they call the "state of nature." (Rawls calls it the "original position.") This is not a historical reality but an imaginary one. It is the hypothetical setting in which, before and outside of political time, individuals are able to consider their relations with one another in the light of principles that apply always and everywhere and whose veracity is demonstrable by reason alone, assuming only certain very basic facts about human

beings (that they have needs, are capable of reasoning, depend on one another, and the like). The goal is to import into the examination of political questions a measure of the axiomatic necessity we expect in mathematical proofs. Hobbes is particularly self-conscious about this. See *Leviathan,* in *The Clarendon Edition of the Works of Thomas Hobbes,* vol. 4, ed. Noel Malcolm (Oxford: Clarendon Press, 1965), 68–70 ("For it is most true that *Cicero* sayth of them somewhere; that there can be nothing so absurd, but may be found in the books of Philosophers. And the reason is manifest. For there is not one of them that begins his ratiocination from the Definitions, or Explications of the names they are to use; which is a method that hath been used onely in Geometry; whose Conclusions have thereby been made indisputable").

19. Plato, *Symposium,* trans. Robin Waterfield (Oxford: Oxford University Press, [1994] 2008), 172a–223d. The whole of Dante's *Commedia* is loosely modeled on the *Symposium.* It describes a journey of ascent, sparked by human love, that culminates in the transfiguring love of God. Dante's pilgrim climbs a ladder, too, like the souls in Diotima's tale. The retirement of Beatrice before God's blinding light near the end of the poem is a magnificent expression of Diotima's principal teaching—that no human love can ever find its fulfillment in anything human.

Ficino's commentary on the *Symposium* repeats this teaching in its essentials. Marsilio Ficino, *On the Nature of Love,* trans. Arthur Farndell (London: Shepheard-Walwyn, 2016). Living in Florence in the second half of the fifteenth century, Ficino was immersed in a culture that celebrated magnificence and display. He was surrounded by works of art. His city, like Socrates' Athens, was brimming with beauty. Ficino was a great connoisseur of beauty. But in his eyes physical beauty in all its forms is only a stepping-stone to something higher that lies beyond the realm of visible grandeur. His commentary on Plato's *Symposium* purports to be the record of a conversation among devotees of the philosopher who had gathered for a dinner in honor of his birthday late in the year 1468.

20. The difference between these two conceptions of love first began to become clear to me years ago when I read Gregory Vlastos's famous essay on the subject. See Vlastos, "The Individual as an Object of Love in Plato," in his *Platonic Studies,* rev. ed. (Princeton: Princeton University Press, 1981), 3–34. Vlastos's essay is wonderfully suggestive. Its implications have been, for me, nearly inexhaustible.

21. The orthodoxy of Church teaching, in both the West and East, emerged in the first five centuries after Christ through a series of conflicts with competing doctrines that were all eventually repudiated as heresies. A large number of these conflicts revolved around the nature of Christ himself—the

so-called Christological debates—and closely related disputes over the triune nature of the God that Christians, like Jews and Muslims, affirm to be one and indivisible (the Trinitarian controversies). Some heretical thinkers claimed that Christ was only human in appearance—that in reality he was wholly divine. Others insisted that he was entirely human and really died on the Cross. Both views had to be rejected to protect the union of God and Man in Christ—a mystery less intelligible than these heretical alternatives but without which the Christian religion is unmoored from the entire system of beliefs and practices that set it apart from every other religious tradition. For details, see Jaroslav Pelikan, *The Christian Tradition: A History of the Development of Doctrine*, vol. 1, *The Emergence of the Catholic Tradition (100–600)* (Chicago: University of Chicago Press, 1971).

22. From Paul Simon's "Graceland": "She comes back to tell me she's gone/As if I didn't know that/As if I didn't know my own bed/As if I'd never noticed/The way she brushed her hair from her forehead."

23. The intellectual and imaginative difficulties presented by this view are immense, perhaps insuperable. They are strikingly apparent in the centuries-long effort by Christian theologians to offer a coherent interpretation of the doctrine of bodily resurrection—of the belief that the faithful shall be raised from the dead in a bodily form. That our bodies in heaven must be like our earthly bodies in *some* respect seems clear. That they cannot be *exactly* like our earthly bodies seems equally clear. The struggle to reconcile these competing ideas is vividly on display in Augustine's convoluted writings on the subject. See Augustine, *The City of God against the Pagans,* trans. R. W. Dyson (Cambridge: Cambridge University Press, 1998), esp. 1111–14 and 1136–52, where Augustine deals with arguments, derived from Cicero and Plato, that earthly bodies cannot be resurrected into heaven. Augustine first contends that when the body is resurrected, it will have the dimensions it attained or would have attained at full maturity. This may mean that features must be added to the body to give it beauty and proportion. He then concedes that the body may instead be resurrected in the form in which it departed earthly life. This brings up, again, a problem he had previously considered but not, it seems, resolved: that of the resurrection of bodies disfigured in death.

24. No philosopher in the last hundred years has better described or more deeply explored the meaning of romantic love than Irish Murdoch. At times, I think, Murdoch fails to distinguish the romantic and Platonic ideals of love as clearly as she might, but her writings remain, for me, a source of encouragement and inspiration. See Iris Murdoch, *The Sovereignty of Good* (New York: Routledge, 2001).

25. Isaiah Berlin offers a particularly insightful account of the intellectual origins of romantic nationalism in *Three Critics of the Enlightenment: Vico,*

Hamann, Herder, ed. Henry Hardy, 2nd ed. (Princeton: Princeton University Press, 2013). The Enlightenment, especially in its French branch, stressed the universality of human experience. It emphasized cosmopolitan values. Against these, the counter-Enlightenment thinkers who are the subject of Berlin's book assigned greater value to the particular historical, cultural, and linguistic experiences that distinguish one nation—and therefore one nation-state—from another. The philosophical champions of nationalism, in the eighteenth and nineteenth centuries, made *individuality* the touchstone of political allegiance, as the novelists of the period did in the realm of personal attachments. This is the sense in which both are "romantic" in spirit.

26. One thinks of Dickens's ruthless caricature of Mrs. Jellyby in *Bleak House* (1853), ed. Stephen Gill (Oxford: Oxford University Press, 1998). Surrounded by her children, who live in squalor and parental neglect, Mrs. Jellyby devotes herself to philanthropic projects meant to raise the condition of the distant and anonymous wretched of the earth.

27. *Jerry Maguire,* directed by Cameron Crowe (Culver City: Sony Pictures, 1996).

28. Franz Kafka, *The Metamorphosis,* trans. Willa Muir and Edwin Muir (New York: Vintage, [1948] 1992). In *The Human Condition* (Chicago: University of Chicago Press, 1958), 184–87, Hannah Arendt describes the vicissitudes of the lifelong campaign to be or become an individual with a unique and unrepeatable biography; see especially chap. 5, on action. She stresses three things. The first is the potential singularity of every human life. We may wind up as conformists, but each human being is, as Arendt says, a "new beginning" with the promise of bringing something altogether original into the world. A second is the narrative unity of every human life. Whatever their disruptions and dislocations, each of our lives is a story with organizing themes. A third is the dependence on others for the meaning of this story itself. What it signifies is not (entirely) for the individual to say. It is up to others to interpret it—to shape it into a story of any kind at all. In this sense, though we are each the hero (the protagonist) of the story of our life, we are not its author. We cannot write it as we choose.

29. Goethe, *Faust,* pt. 1, trans. Peter Salm, rev. ed. (New York: Bantam Books, 1967), l. 1700.

30. Thomas Mann, *Buddenbrooks: The Decline of a Family,* trans. John Woods (New York: Vintage, 1994), 730–31.

31. *Places in the Heart,* directed by Robert Benton (Culver City: Tristar Pictures, 1984). The last episode of the third season of the Israeli television series *Shtisel* concludes with a similar image. The father of the family, Shulem Shtisel, is sitting at a table with his son and brother. His relations with both are strained. He quotes Isaac Bashevis Singer: "The dead don't go anywhere.

They're all here. Each man is a cemetery. An actual cemetery, in which lie all our grandmothers and grandfathers, the father and mother, the wife, the child. Everyone is here all the time." And then, magically, they reappear. The entire family, living and dead, are gathered in the kitchen, eating and talking—heaven as a family reunion. *Shtisel,* directed by Alon Zingman (Netflix, 2013–21).

3
Illusions of Fulfillment

1. Sigmund Freud, *Civilization and Its Discontents* in *The Standard Edition of the Complete Psychological Works of Sigmund Freud,* ed. and trans. James Strachey, vol. 21 (New York: W. W. Norton, 1961), 72.

2. Augustine offers a classic formulation of this view. "Nor did You precede time by any time; because then You would not precede all times. But in the excellency of an ever-present eternity, You precede all times past, and survive all future times, because they are future, and when they have come they will be past; but 'You are the same, and Your years shall have no end.' Your years neither go nor come; but ours both go and come, that all may come. . . . You have made all time; and before all times You are, nor in any time was there not time." *The Confessions,* trans. J. G. Pilkington (Edinburgh: T. and T. Clark, 1876), 31.

3. Whether the doctrine of divine creation is compatible with the belief that the world has no beginning in time but is coeval with God's eternal existence was a subject of fierce debate among theologians in all three Abrahamic traditions. Compare, for example, Avicenna, *The Metaphysics of the Healing,* trans. Michael E. Marmura (Provo: Brigham Young University Press, 2005); Maimonides, *A Guide to the Perplexed,* trans. M. Friedlander (Abingdon, U.K.: Routledge and Kegan Paul, 1956); Aquinas, "On Being and Essence," trans. Robert T. Miller, in *Internet Medieval Source Book* (New York: Fordham University Center for Medieval Studies, 1997). Those who held that a belief in the coeternity of the world is compatible with the doctrine of creation did so because, in their view, even if the world is everlasting, it depends for its existence on God, whose being is necessary and not contingent—as that of the world, whether everlasting or not, is by its very nature as a created thing. This position exploits the distinction between the two senses of eternity noted in chapter 2.

4. The spirit of otherworldliness is particularly strong in Christianity and Islam. The first, after its messianic beginnings, settled down and made peace with the world. Hopes for a second coming faded; churches and bish-

ops acquired an authority in mundane affairs. But otherworldly longings remained strong. They inspired the monastic movement (which eventually settled down too) and the Protestant Reformation, born in a mood of disgust with the worldly extravagance of the papal court and lax practices of the Church in general.

Islam made peace with the world even more quickly. Within a century after the death of the Prophet, it had become a great imperial power. In very general terms, the whole of Islamic law—one the great expressions of Islamic civilization—represents an accommodation to worldly realities. Yet over the centuries, countless theologians, mystics, and reformers have reminded the faithful that their true home is not in this world. They have called them back to a purity of thought and worship whose energies are concentrated on the hopes of the world to come. The writings of Maududi and Qutub, and the radical movements that have swept the Islamic world in the name of their purifying ambitions, offer a contemporary example. Maududi's most extensive work is his six-volume *Tafhim-ul-Quran*, or *Towards Understanding the Qur'ān*, trans. Zafar Ishaq Ansari (Villa Park, Ill.: Islamic Foundation, 1995), an exegesis of the Qur'an with an eye to modern problems. He was a prolific writer of books and pamphlets, among them *The Concept of Jihad in Islam*, trans. Syed Rahatallah Shah and ed. Syed Firasat Shah (Lahore: Idara Tarjuman ul Qur'an, 2017), and *Towards Understanding Islam*, trans. Khurshid Ahmad (Villa Park, Ill.: Islamic Foundation, 1974). Qutub admired Maududi and refers to Maududi in his best-known work, *Milestones*, trans. Ahmad Zaki Hammad (Indianapolis: American Trust, 1990), and in his own multi-volume commentary on the Qur'an, *In the Shade of the Qur'ān*, trans. and ed. Adil Salahi (Villa Park, Ill.: Islamic Foundation, 2003). See also Jan-Peter Hartung, *A System of Life: Mawdūdī and the Ideologisation of Islam* (Oxford: Oxford University Press, 2014); John Calvert, *Sayyid Qutb and the Origins of Radical Islamism* (New York: Columbia University Press, 2010); Irfan Ahmad, "Genealogy of the Islamic State: Reflections on Maududi's Political Thought and Islamism," *Journal of the Royal Anthropological Institute* 15.1 (2009): 145–62.

Judaism is the outlier. It has been a worldly religion of laws from the start. And yet—paradoxically—though most at home in the world, of the three Abrahamic religions it is the one in which a spirit of homelessness has penetrated most deeply. For post-exilic Jews, who have been wandering for two millennia, the idea of a homecoming, which once meant something practical, has been transmuted into a goal as unattainable on earth as the heaven of Christians and Muslims. Religious Jews who opposed the establishment of the State of Israel did so, in part, because they feared a conflation of religious and worldly values—which is not to say that the worldly arguments for the creation of the State of Israel are unconvincing. I myself find them compelling.

5. Augustine expressed his views about predestination with increasing rigor in the last years of his life. He presents them with uncompromising severity in his controversy with the British monk Pelagius, who stood by the claim that human beings possess a real if modest degree of freedom. Augustine treats the thought of Pelagius and his followers extensively—from *On the Merits and Remission of Sins and on the Baptism of Infants,* written in 412, through *The Predestination of the Saints* and *The Gift of Perseverance,* each written in 429, the year before Augustine died. See *The Anti-Pelagian Works of St. Augustine,* trans. Peter Holmes, vol. 1 in *The Works of Aurelius Augustine,* ed. Marcus Dods (Edinburgh: T. and T. Clark, 1872), and *Answer to the Pelagians IV: To the Monks of Hadrumetum and Provence,* trans. Roland J. Teske, in *The Works of St. Augustine,* pt. 1, vol. 26, ed. John E. Rotelle (New York: New City Press, 1999), esp. 179–81 and 196–98. Luther defends the Augustinian view in his famous exchange with Erasmus, whom he characterized as a latter-day Pelagian. Luther, *On the Bondage of the Will,* trans. J. I. Packer and O. R. Johnston (London: J. Clarke, 1957).

6. Augustine, *The City of God against the Pagans,* trans. R. W. Dyson (Cambridge: Cambridge University Press, 1998), 861–63.

7. Plato, *Republic,* trans. Paul Shorey, in *Collected Dialogues of Plato,* ed. Edith Hamilton and Huntington Cairns (Princeton: Princeton University Press, 1980), 514a–517a.

8. Jacob Klein gives an extended and enlightening account of this power and of the role it plays in human life in *A Commentary on Plato's Meno* (Chicago: University of Chicago Press, 1998). Klein's book suggests a way of thinking about the central arguments of the *Republic* that changed my view of that work forever.

9. Baudelaire, "The Albatross," trans. Richard Wilbur, in Wilbur, *Collected Poems, 1943–2004* (New York: Harvest, 2004), 55.

10. The *Symposium* tells us that Socrates sometimes fell into a speechless trance and remained in it for a considerable time. *Symposium,* trans. Robin Waterfield (Oxford: Oxford University Press, [1994] 2008), 174d–175d. This is unusual for anyone, but especially for Socrates, who delighted in the company of others and spent most of his time conversing with them. Where is Socrates in these speechless interludes? Plato's readers are led to suppose that his teacher was, from time to time, transported to a visionary state like the one Socrates himself describes in the *Republic* as the culmination of the philosopher's long upward climb to a knowledge of the Form of the Good.

11. This point is elaborated in convincing detail in John Herman Ran-

dall's *Aristotle* (New York: Columbia University Press, 1960), a classic work of lasting value.

12. Aristotle, *De Anima,* trans. J. A. Smith, in *The Works of Aristotle,* ed. W. D. Ross, vol. 3 (Oxford: Clarendon Press, 1931), 415a–b.

13. Aristotle, *Physics,* trans. Robin Waterfield (Oxford: Oxford University Press, 1996), 219b.

14. See Aristotle, *On the Heavens,* trans. W. K. C. Guthrie, Loeb Classical Library 338 (Cambridge: Harvard University Press, 1939), 271a; Aristotle, *Parts of Animals,* trans. A. L. Peck and E. S. Forster, Loeb Classical Library 323 (Cambridge: Harvard University Press, 1937), 641a; Aristotle, *Politics,* ed. R. F. Stalley and trans. Ernest Baker (Oxford: Oxford University Press, 2009), 1253a.

15. Aristotle, *Metaphysics,* trans. Hugh Tredennick (Cambridge: Harvard University Press, 1933), 1072a–1073b.

16. Aristotle, *Nicomachean Ethics,* trans. Martin Ostwald (Indianapolis: Bobbs-Merrill, 1962), 1098a.

17. Karl Marx, *Capital,* ed. Frederick Engels, vol. 1 (New York: Modern Library, 1906), 198.

18. Aristotle, *Politics,* 1253a.

19. Ibid., 1302a–1304a.

20. Aristotle, *De Anima,* 425b, 427a–b.

21. Aristotle, *Nicomachean Ethics,* 1177b–1178a.

22. Ibid., 1140a 4–1141b 2.

23. I have sometimes been told that my views resemble those held by the followers of one or another of the Eastern religions. I can neither confirm nor deny it, as lawyers sometimes say. My knowledge of the Eastern religions is too thin to permit me to make the comparison.

I concede that the position at which I have arrived is Eurocentric in two ways. It has grown out of my study of works in the Western tradition and been shaped by reflection on peculiarly Western experiences—most important, the new science of nature, which, beginning in sixteenth-century Europe, has transformed our understanding of the world and produced the regime of scientific research that is now a globally ubiquitous phenomenon. I do claim for my ideas a universal application. I say that I am offering a portrait of the human condition. Whether the parochialism of my education, of the texts and experiences that have provoked my reflections, compromises the universality of my ideas is not for me to say.

24. Baruch Spinoza, *Ethics,* in *The Collected Works of Spinoza,* trans. Edwin Curley (Princeton: Princeton University Press, 1985), 5p42s.

25. Plotinus, *The Enneads,* trans. Stephen Mackenna (Burdett, N.Y.: Larson, 1992), I.3.2–3.

4

Prospects of Joy

1. Leo Hamalian and Edmond Volpe, eds., *Ten Modern Short Novels* (New York: G. P. Putnam's Sons, 1958), 643.

2. Philip Larkin, "Church Going," in *Collected Poems*, ed. Anthony Thwaite (London: Marvell, 1988), 97–98.

3. The path I follow in my thinking might be described in the following way. *First* I ask, "What does it mean to be a human being, not at one time or place rather than another, but everywhere and always? How shall we think about the human condition in general?" My answer to this first question has been influenced by many thinkers, but above all by Kant.

Kant portrays our condition as that of a "finite rational being." *Critique of Practical Reason*, in *Practical Philosophy*, ed. and trans. Mary J. Gregor (Cambridge: Cambridge University Press, 1996), 166. Rationality is the power of abstraction. It allows us to see events, as they occur in the stream of time, from a point of view outside it. More exactly, reason is this point of view itself. Finitude is our confinement to the stream of time—the fact that we are carried along by it even while we "watch" it from outside. The two together make us the beings we are—human beings, caught in time yet beyond it, mortal and aware that we are. Kant takes me this far.

But then a *second* question arises. "What must the world as a whole be like for the experience of being human to be possible at all?" That we *actually* have this experience is obvious. Is there anything about the world that must *necessarily* be true, for the *possibility* of our having the experience we do to be intelligible to us—that is, something other than a brute fact we must accept but can neither understand nor explain? Kant calls questions of this sort "transcendental." An answer to this second, transcendental question about the human condition carries us to the outermost limits of human understanding. It does not, of course, allow us to step outside our condition, but it does enable us to comprehend it.

Kant was hesitant to take up this second question. He thought of it as a metaphysical or theological problem and viewed his own "critical" philosophy as a permanent barrier to inquiries of this sort. To the extent he did pursue it, Kant's reflections led him to a view about the nature of reality—the world as a whole—that was still shaped by the Christian assumption that the world has a supernatural ground or cause. I am convinced this view cannot provide an answer to the transcendental question of how human experience is even conceivable. It is still wedded to the belief, which all the Abrahamic religions share, that an omnipotent God can and must rescue us from the travails of our condition.

The only satisfying answer, I believe, is the one that Spinoza offers in the *Ethics*, in *The Collected Works of Spinoza*, trans. Edwin Curley (Princeton: Princeton University Press, 1985), 408–620. Spinoza's God is nothing apart from the world. It is the world itself—more exactly, its infinite power and intelligibility. This God, unlike Kant's, promises no relief from the deep disappointment of the human condition. But it does allow us to explain how such disappointment is possible at all and why it is accompanied by the possibility of endless joy—indeed, why these two, disappointment and joy, are necessarily joined. In a word, Spinoza's theology provides the best—in my view, the only—foundation for Kant's philosophical anthropology. It puts Kant's account of the human condition on a secure cosmic foundation. More than this we cannot ask.

4. Spinoza defines God as "a being absolutely infinite, i.e., a substance consisting of an infinity of attributes, of which each one expresses an eternal and infinite essence." *Ethics* 1d6. Spinoza's God is "the face of the whole universe, which, although varying in infinite ways, yet remains always the same." See *Spinoza: The Letters*, trans. Samuel Shirley (Indianapolis: Hackett, 1995), Ep64. It is distinguished from the Gods of Athens and Jerusalem by its combination of inherence and infinity. Unlike the God of Abraham, the God of the *Ethics* is *in* the world. More exactly, it *is* the world. More exactly still, it is the world *seen in a certain light* (under what Spinoza calls the "aspect of eternity"). God's inherence is not limited, though, to a particular department or dimension of reality, in the way Aristotle's God is. To be sure, our *understanding* of it is limited. But the further we probe, the more divinity we discover. There is no end to it. The reality, being, and power of Spinoza's God is *infinite*, like that of Abraham's God, who exists beyond the world and time.

5. Aristotle, *Metaphysics*, trans. Hugh Tredennick (Cambridge: Harvard University Press, 1933), 982b.

6. The experience of finding the world accessible to understanding, never completely but always more so than at the present moment, is one of the inspirations for the philosophy of science developed by the American philosopher and scientist Charles Sanders Peirce. Peirce's writings are scattered and difficult. The difficulty is made greater by Peirce's invention of a number of idiosyncratic terms (*abduction, pragmaticism, methodeutic, tychism,* and the like).

Still, Peirce's work as a practicing scientist made him exquisitely sensitive both to the endlessly progressive character of scientific discovery and to the impossibility of ever reaching the goal toward which every scientist strives. Peirce is one of the great philosophers of modern research science, so different from the form of scientific inquiry that Aristotle, who was also a first-rate scientist, had in mind when he constructed his own philosophy of science. For a sense of Peirce's views, see "How to Make Our Ideas Clear" and "Man's Glassy Essence," in *Chance, Love, and Logic: Philosophical Essays*, ed. Morris R. Cohen (Lincoln: University of Nebraska Press, [1923] 1998), 32–60 and 238–66. Peirce was not a Spinozist. He disavowed the kind of uncompromising determinism that Spinoza defends. He was, however, drawn to and influenced by the writings of both Kant and Hegel. Kant's notion of a "regulative principle" had, in particular, an especially large influence on Peirce's thinking.

7. Descartes, *Meditations on First Philosophy*, in *The Philosophical Works of Descartes*, trans. Elizabeth Haldane and G. R. T. Ross, vol. 1 (Cambridge: Cambridge University Press, 1967), 183. Skepticism comes in many varieties, of which Descartes's is only one. There is, for example, Sextus Empiricus's ancient version of it and Hume's "more *mitigated* skepticism." Sextus Empiricus, *Outlines of Scepticism*, ed. and trans. Julia Annas and Jonathan Barnes (Cambridge: Cambridge University Press, 2000), and Hume, *An Enquiry Concerning Human Understanding*, ed. L. A. Selby-Bigge and P. H. Nidditch (Oxford: Clarendon Press, 1975), 161. None of the skeptical doubts raised by any of these philosophers, though, impugns the *reality* of the experience of scientific progress. What they challenge is the way we most commonly *explain* this experience: by asserting that our ideas accurately represent the world as it is in itself.

Kant short-circuits all these arguments. He concedes that we can never know the world, as it is independent of our representations. But our experience is unintelligible, he says, except on the assumption that events are connected according to laws. Remove this assumption, he argues, and experience itself disappears. This is Kant's transcendental rejoinder to philosophical skepticism—which simultaneously undermines all forms of dogmatism, that is, every philosophy that depends on the assumption that we are indeed able to grasp the world as it is in itself. In this way, Kant thought, his new "critical" philosophy kills two ancient birds with a single stone.

8. See Ernst Cassirer, *Determinism and Indeterminism in Modern Physics*, trans. O. T. Benfey (New Haven: Yale University Press, 1956), and Werner Heisenberg, *Philosophical Problems of Quantum Physics*, trans. F. C. Hayes (Woodbridge, Conn.: Ox Bow Press, 1979). Kristian Camilleri's "Indeterminacy and the Limits of Classical Concepts: The Transformation of Heisenberg's Thought," *Perspectives on Science* 15.2 (2007): 178–201, updates Heisenberg's and Cassirer's discussions of indeterminacy. Tim Maudlin's *Philosophy of Physics: Quantum Theory* (Princeton: Princeton University Press, 2019) is a helpful, if idiosyncratic, introduction.

9. "Let any one *define* a cause, without comprehending, as a part of the definition, a *necessary connexion,* with its effect; and let him show distinctly the origin of the idea, expressed by the definition; and I shall readily give up the whole controversy." Hume, *An Enquiry Concerning Human Understanding,* 95–96. Kant says something similar in *Prolegomena to Any Future Metaphysics,* ed. and trans. Gary Hatfield, rev. ed. (Cambridge: Cambridge University Press, 2004), 62–65.

10. On the uncertainty principle, see Werner Heisenberg, *The Physical Principles of the Quantum Theory,* trans. Carl Eckart and Frank C. Hoyt (Chicago: University of Chicago Press, 1930), 20. Thomas Young's famous double-slit experiment was performed more than a hundred years before the first quantum theories were advanced. It is said to demonstrate the phenomenon of superposition. In Young's experiment, light passing through two parallel slits on a plate creates on a screen behind the plate four distinct bands at once. The resulting pattern of interference is offered as evidence of the fact that light can exist simultaneously in different quantum states. Mark P. Silverman describes this experiment and others in *Quantum Superposition: Counterintuitive Consequences of Coherence, Entanglement, and Interference* (Berlin: Springer, 2008).

For its part, "decoherence destroys superpositions." Wojciech Zurek, "Decoherence and the Transition from Quantum to Classical," *Physics Today* 44.10 (1991): 44. "Decoherence" results from the fact that "macroscopic quantum systems are never isolated from their environments." Coherent quantum relations can always "leak out" and become incoherent. Ibid., 37. Because a closed quantum system cannot be measured, decoherence is presumably a feature of any of our observations of such a system. H. Dieter Zeh pioneered decoherence theory in the 1970s; Zurek significantly developed the idea in the 1980s.

11. On reconciling quantum theory with general relativity through a theory of quantum gravity, see Claus Kiefer, *Quantum Gravity,* 2nd ed. (Oxford: Oxford University Press, 2007). Philip R. Sloan and Brandon Fogel, eds., *Creating a Physical Biology: The Three-Man Paper and Early Molecular Biology* (Chicago: University of Chicago Press, 2011), describes the early ambition of molecular genetics to bring new theories in physics to bear on biology and charts the result of this revolution. See also Maurizio Meloni and Giuseppe Testa, "Scrutinizing the Epigenetics Revolution," *BioSocieties* 9 (2014): 431–56.

12. Isaac Newton, *The Principia,* trans. I. Bernard Cohen and Anne Whitman with Julia Budenz (Berkeley: University of California Press, 1999), 940–43.

13. Einstein thought "science without religion is lame, religion without science is blind." "Science and Religion," in *Ideas and Opinions*, ed. Sonja Bargmann, rev. ed. (New York: Three Rivers Press, 1982), 46. Einstein's religion was not founded, though, on belief in a "personal god." He said, "I believe in Spinoza's God who reveals himself in the orderly harmony of what exists, not in a God who concerns himself with the fates and actions of human beings." "Einstein Believes in Spinoza's God," *New York Times,* April 25, 1929. See Michel Paty, "Einstein and Spinoza," trans. Michel Paty and Robert S. Cohen, in *Spinoza and the Sciences*, ed. Marjorie Grene and Debra Nails (Dordrecht, Netherlands: Reidel, 1986), 267–302.

14. Aristotle, *Physics*, trans. Robin Waterfield (Oxford: Oxford University Press, 1996), 202b 31–208a.

15. Aristotle, *Nicomachean Ethics*, trans. Martin Ostwald (Indianapolis: Bobbs-Merrill, 1962), 1094b 13.

16. See Stephen Hawking and Leonard Mlodinow, *The Grand Design* (New York: Random House, 2009), 9 ("Each universe has many possible histories and many possible states at later times. . . . Only a very few would allow creatures like us to exist. Thus our presence selects out from this vast array only those universes that are compatible with our existence. Although we are puny and insignificant on the scale of the cosmos, this makes us in a sense the lords of creation"); Stuart Kauffman, *At Home in the Universe: The Search for the Laws of Self-Organization and Complexity* (Oxford: Oxford University Press, 1995), 8 ("Laws of complexity spontaneously generate much of the order of the natural world. . . . Profound order is being discovered in large, complex, and apparently random systems. I believe that this emergent order underlies not only the origin of life itself, but much of the order seen in organisms today").

17. Virginia Woolf, *To the Lighthouse* (1927), ed. David Bradshaw (Oxford: Oxford University Press, 2006), 170.

18. Spinoza, *Ethics*, 2p29c.

19. Hans Blumenberg is an extraordinarily acute observer of the dialectical process through which, beginning in the thirteenth century and leading to and beyond the threshold of the modern age, the attributes of the supernatural creator God of the Christian religion were transferred to the world itself. His grasp of the theological background and of the scientific methods and secular philosophies that sought to meet the challenge that late medieval nominalism bequeathed to its successors is without compare. See Blumenberg, *The Legitimacy of the Modern Age*, trans. Robert M. Wallace (Cambridge: MIT Press, 1983), esp. pt. IV.

20. Spinoza, *Ethics*, 3p11s.

21. Ibid., 5p41s. See also Spinoza, *Short Treatise on God, Man, and His*

Well-Being, in *Collected Works,* 2.XXVI.4 ("This is as silly as if a fish (which cannot live outside water) should say: if no eternal life is to come to me after this life in the water, I want to leave the water for the land").

22. Henry James, preface to *The Portrait of a Lady* (1881) (New York: Modern Library, 2002), xxi; Aristotle, *Poetics,* ed. and trans. Stephen Halliwell, Loeb Classical Library 199 (Cambridge: Harvard University Press, 1995), 1450a 39.

23. See my *Confessions of a Born-Again Pagan* (New Haven: Yale University Press, 2016), 900–905.

24. Eric Karpeles explores Proust's painterly sensibility, and his particular interest in Vermeer and Titian, in *Paintings in Proust: A Visual Companion to* In Search of Lost Time (London: Thames and Hudson, 2008). See also the essays collected in *Proust and the Arts,* ed. Christie McDonald and François Proulx (Cambridge: Cambridge University Press, 2015), esp. Susan Ricci Stebbins's "'Those blessed days': Ruskin, Proust, and Carpaccio in Venice." Of his own novel Proust said, "My book is a painting." Karpeles, *Paintings in Proust,* 10.

25. *Leaves of Grass* is a celebration of the uniqueness of every individual being, "no two alike, and every one good." Walt Whitman, *Leaves of Grass* (1891–92 ed.), in *Walt Whitman: Poetry and Prose,* ed. Justin Kaplan (New York: Library of America, 1982), 32. On idiocrasy, see Walt Whitman, *Democratic Vistas,* ed. Ed Folsom (Iowa City: University of Iowa Press [1871] 2010), 38, 57.

Acknowledgments

I have been thinking about these matters for most of my life. I have accumulated a lifetime of debts along the way.

To my wife, Nancy, I owe thanks for her contributions to my thinking about so many subjects, and her helpful, humorous depreciation of my tendency to lose myself in labyrinths like this one. If I know anything about romantic love, it is on Nancy's account.

To my dearest friends I am thankful for the joy of our lives together. This includes the joy of thinking but so much else besides. David Bromwich, Steven Smith, Bryan Garsten, Roya Hakakian, Michael Della Rocca, Moshe Halbertal, Paul Kahn, Bruce Ackerman, Daniel Markovits, Rick and Jane Levin, Adam Glick and Denise Scruton, Jed Rubenfeld and Amy Chua: my life is inconceivable without them.

I am grateful to my friends and fellow fishermen José de Lasa and Jack Lynch for our time together on the water, looking for fish and talking about God. They have been generous in welcoming a disbeliever on board.

To Hannah Carrese, Yale Law School '22, I owe thanks for her spirited and imaginative help in preparing the manuscript of the book for publication.

Jennifer Banks, my editor at Yale University Press, has been a wonderful ally from the start.

Finally, to my hero and friend Owen Fiss I owe a special measure of thanks for his encouraging and cautionary words regarding the form and substance of this book. His contributions were so many that, by the end, I felt he ought to be the book's coauthor—except for the fact that the ideas expressed here are, as they say, those of the author alone, and I have good reason to believe that Owen disagrees with many of them. I dedicate the book to him as a heartfelt second best.

Block Island, May 2021

Index